brain storming sessions at your home and requests for, "that great new recipe we had last week", it will be a success.

Pork as a type of meat and the preparation of the various cuts of pork are changing more than any type of meat. You won't want to be left behind in pork fashions. If your character traits include curiosity and the courage to try the new and different and yet retain the tried and true, this book was written for you. S-o-o

To market, to market, etc.

Gertrude Kable

Gertrude Kable,
Manager Checkerboard Kitchens, Consumer Services

Library of Congress Catalog Card Number: 70-39482

07-051159-4

123456789 DODO 798765432

Help from the following organizations is gratefully acknowledged:
Elanco Products Company, National Livestock and Meat Board, and National Pork Council.

American Heirloom Pork Cook Book

From Checkerboard Kitchens

McGRAW-HILL BOOK COMPANY
New York   St. Louis   San Francisco   Düsseldorf
London   Mexico   Sydney   Toronto

table of contents

the story of pork

Through the ages, pork has been an important food all over the world. The Chinese and Romans were as proud of their special hams as are Americans, French and others today.

Chinese hams were cured with yellow wine brine, smoked over tea leaves and dried in the wind. The first country hams were processed by the Romans in Gaul. Curing and smoking of meat were practiced in such diverse parts of the world because these were the only methods of meat preservation.

The Spanish and English brought hogs to the new world, which could feed themselves by rooting in the forest and were natural home and village scavengers as well as clearers of undergrowth. The standard fare of the pioneers and settlers was salt pork. Occasional game birds or fish were the only relief.

Cincinnati processed so many hogs in the early 1800's that it was called, "Porkopolis". Pork processing was one of that city's main industries.

Why were pigs preferred to cattle or sheep? They could pretty well take care of themselves and even help to care for man. Hogs were ready for butchering sooner than cattle and pork tasted better when salted, pickled or smoked. In the days before refrigeration was standard equipment, the salting of meat was very important.

Pork was even responsible for two widely used slang expressions. "Pork Barrel", referred to government appropriations for patronage. Early in the 19th century, the shilling in Ireland and England and the dime in the United States were referred to as hogs. To spend it all in one place was to go, "whole hog".

Until the last few decades, to look prosperous was to be heavy. Therefore extra fat on pork was not only acceptable, it was a plus factor. With the newer knowledge in medical and nutrition science overweight is frowned upon and the hog, ever the adaptable, has been bred to be a very lean animal.

This new pork is now on the market and has just about replaced the heavier product. What will be the difference to you? You can count on fewer calories and more nutrition per serving. Most important of all, new lean pork has an even better flavor and is rapidly becoming more popular than ever.

the place of pork in the modern diet

Meats and dairy products are the best sources of high quality protein. As such, they are important to build and repair body tissues (bones, teeth, muscles, skin, blood, hair, etc.), and to supply important vitamins and minerals. They are especially rich in the B vitamins that are necessary for the body to use food, for good appetites and skin, as well as for general well-being. Pork is also a good source of other vitamins and minerals including iron. Pork liver has about 3 times as much available iron as any other food.

The new lean pork has more protein and less fat. Naturally, it also has lower calories. There are about 36% fewer calories, which means that most major cuts are less than 250 calories per 3-1/2 ounce serving.

It is delightful in both flavor and texture for any of the three daily meals. Pork can now be prepared by all methods including broiling and when roasted, is cooked a shorter length of time to make it juicier. Don't forget—studies show that pork is at least 96% digestible.

the four food group guide to daily eating

Meat group—2 or more servings daily. Meat, poultry, fish, eggs with dried peas, beans and nuts as alternatives.

Milk group—2 to 4 glasses or ice cream or cheese can supply part of milk.

Cereal and Bread group 4 or more servings daily.

Fruits and Vegetables group 4 or more servings daily. Include 1 citrus fruit. Serve dark green leafy or yellow vegetable often.

pork cuts	cooking method	cooking time	price range
Fresh Ham	Roast-oven rotisserie	Long	Med.
Sirloin	Roast-oven rotisserie	Long	Med.
Center Loin	Roast-oven rotisserie	Long	Higher
Blade Loin	Roast-oven rotisserie	Long	Med. to Low
Shoulder Picnic	Roast-oven rotisserie Pot Roast	Long	Med. to Low
Cushion	Roast-oven	Long	Med. to Low
Boston Butt	Roast Pot Roast	Long	Med. to Low
Arm	Roast	Long	Med. to Low
Crown Roast	Roast	Long	High
Tenderloin	Roast-Braise BBQ	Short to Med.	Med. to Fancy High
Chops and Steaks			
Loin	Bake-BBQ-Braise	Med.	Med. to High
Sirloin	Bake-BBQ-Braise	Med.	Med. to High
Rib	Bake-BBQ-Braise	Med.	Med.
Butterfly	Bake-BBQ-Braise	Med.	High
Blade	Bake-BBQ-Braise	Med. to Short	Med. to Low
Arm	Bake-BBQ-Braise	Med. to Short	Med. to Low
Pork Cutlet	Braise	Short	Low
Spareribs	Bake-BBQ	Long	Med. to Low
Country Style Backbone	Bake-BBQ	Long	Low
Pork Sausage	Braise-Fry	Med.	Med.
Liver	Braise-Bake	Med.	Low
Brains	Braise	Med. to Short	Low
Heart	Braise-Bake	Long	Low
Kidney	Braise-Bake	Long	Low
Feet	Braise-Simmer	Long	Low
Knuckles	Braise-Simmer	Long	Low
Ham	Bake-BBQ-Fry-Broil	Short to Long	Low to High
Bacon	Bake-Fry-Broil	Short	Low to Med.
Canadian Style Bacon	Bake-Fry-Broil	Short to Med.	Med. to High
Smoked Jowl	Simmer-Fry	Med. to Short	Low
Pork Feet	Simmer	Long	Low

ROASTS

Fresh Picnic	Smoked Picnic	Rolled Fresh Picnic	Boston Butt	Rolled Boston Butt
Smoked Boneless Shoulder Butt	Arm Roast	Rib Loin	Blade Loin	Center Loin
Sirloin	Leg (Fresh or Smoked Ham)	Crown Roast	Canadian Style Bacon	

OTHER CUTS

Country Style Backbone

CHOPS AND STEAKS

Blade	Rib	Loin	Blade Steak	Spareribs
Sirloin	Butterfly	Tenderloin	Smoked Ham Center Slice	Cutlet

how to use this book

Our aim is to supply pork information. We hope that you will use this book as:

A reference book for your questions.

A meal planner. Every recipe will have a menu.

A party book. Each recipe includes garnishes as well as menus.

A budget minder.

A frustration chaser. Substitutions are on the inside back cover and a list of herbs is in the back.

A record book. The wide margins are for you to make your notes and keep your records. This is an heirloom cook book.

A guide to busy day tips.

Variations: Every cook likes to use her own creative twists in recipes and we agree. However, aside from minor changes in seasoning, it will be easier for you to familiarize yourself with the recipe by trying it as written first.

Level Measurements: All recipes are based on level measurements; dry measuring cups for dry ingredients and liquid measuring cups for liquid ingredients. There is a difference.

Oven Temperatures: These may account for the failure or success of your meal. It's a good idea to use an oven thermometer.

Meat Thermometer: Since no two pieces of meat are exactly alike, you will find that the only way to serve delicious, tender and juicy meat every time will be to use a meat thermometer. It will tell you exactly when the roast is ready to come out of the oven. It costs money and flavor to overcook meat.

Glossary: Don't bother to reach for the dictionary if you don't recognize a word; look in the back of the book in the glossary.

Pan Size: This is important in some recipes to the extent of complete failure. Usually, in the case of meat, it simply means a lack of proper browning or, if the pan is too small, a spattered oven. Neither is very appealing.

Yields: The number of servings given for a recipe means the number of portions not the number of people served. A portion will be determined by the recipe, the occasion and what else will be served with the recipe. A boneless portion of a roast is considered to be 3-1/2 ounces. A stew will also include a half cup of vegetable and a potato. A luncheon portion will be smaller than a dinner serving. Ham and beans will be larger because a salad and bread will be the only accompaniment. Isn't that the way you do it for your family? Of course you will know how many portions each will eat.

about managing that budget... attractively

Despite the fact that the average consumer spends less than 5% of disposable income (after taxes) for meat it is still the most expensive single item in the food budget. Meat is also one of the main protein sources. Therefore, we must budget carefully to be able to get the most meat and the best quality for our money.

1. Take inventory of leftovers, cupboards, refrigerator and freezer before making your shopping list.

2. Watch for sales and specials. If you have a freezer, plan to buy meat when it is on sale for a special price. Be sure you know what you are buying.

3. Know your quality and know your prices. If you're a new homemaker or new to an area, it might be worth your while to chart prices for a month or two.

4. Get to know your meat man. This means shopping when the store isn't crowded, if possible. He will be happy to help if he has the time and knows your needs. He does have some limitations. For instance, a large store may not be able to grind one or two pounds of meat for you because such a small amount would be lost in a huge grinder.

5. Shop from a list that has been made from the next week's menus. Be open minded. As you carefully inspect the prices and quality in the *entire* meat case, take advantage of any low prices that will fit your needs.

6. If you don't recognize certain cuts, ask (or read further in this book). Ask or read also, how to cook them.

7. If you have a freezer or a friend who will share it, buy a whole ham and ask the meat man to cut it. The hock, the skin and the bones (when you've finished the rest of the ham) are great for navy bean or split pea soup. Several center slices will cost a lot less this way. The butt and shank pieces are delicious for roasts and sandwiches. Even a family of two can use a ham within 2 or 3 months this way. It will maintain quality for this length of time if properly wrapped and frozen. Larger cuts of fresh meat can be handled the same way.

8. In general, a rule of thumb is, the larger the ham or roast, the smaller the proportion of bone to meat.

9. One of the most important rules of successful budgeting is, *don't waste* anything. Cook what will be eaten. If there are leftovers, freeze them, cream them or make them into soups, salads, sandwiches or spreads and dips. Don't let them become senior citizens of the refrigerator before they get pitched.

continued on next page

10. Suit the quality to the purpose. For instance, shoulder meat will be just as suitable for a salad or a ragoût as a loin or tenderloin, and is much cheaper. The same is true for the ingredients for meat dishes. Hand packed canned tomatoes are lovely for salads but less fancy ones will be just as attractive for stews, soups or for some casseroles.

11. Count the cost per serving, not the cost per pound. An expensive boneless cut may really be cheaper per serving than a less expensive cut with much bone or gristle that must be discarded.

12. Decide which is more important in your way of life—money saving or time saving, and buy accordingly.

13. Keep records—of proper amounts, good buys, good cuts, good recipes, good combinations. They will help both your time and money budgets. Records do wonders for the peace of mind, too.

14. Use imagination. What if you haven't heard of that combination before? It will help make meals adventuresome for the family, also.

selecting pork...in general

Inspection: Pork is inspected for wholesomeness just like any other meat. Be sure to check for the stamp indicating that the meat has had federal, state or city inspection.

Grading: Since pork is cut from young animals, tenderness is not usually a factor. The entire carcass is graded by the government on the basis of the amount of lean and fat, but the public doesn't see that grade on the wholesale and retail cuts.

Branding: Hogs have and are being bred to be leaner than in the past. Some of the large meat packers are now branding this special pork by supplying small stickers for the retailers to place on individual chops, loin roasts and shoulder cuts. There isn't nearly enough of this very fancy pork so don't blame your meat dealer if he hasn't been able to get enough, yet.

Identification: In the meantime, how can you identify top quality pork cuts? The color is pale pink; the texture is fine and has specks of fat through the lean. Meat men call that marbling. As far as you're concerned, it means juicy, flavorful meat. Top quality pork is not watery. Watery pork shrinks much more than quality pork. You don't need that. Both fresh, and smoked and cured pork are so tasty and nutritious that every homemaker, we could go even further and say every consumer, should be able to recognize and select high quality pork cuts. They taste that good!

selection and economy of individual cuts

Bone is the key word in the identification of the various cuts and to some extent, the economy. Fortunately the bone structure is the same in pork, lamb, beef and veal. When you learn one, you learn them all. The names may vary slightly as in ham, leg or round, or picnic, chuck or shoulder, but that isn't too difficult. In general, with the exception of veal, the cooking methods are the same, too. The economy of the individual cuts is determined by several things. The more difficult it is to carve and the more bone there is in proportion to lean, the less desirable the cut is, and hence the less expensive it is. Spareribs in summer is probably the main exception. The law of supply and demand also determines the cost of the cuts. This is why meats that require long cooking periods are more popular and more expensive in winter. Spareribs and steaks are more popular and usually cost more in summer when they can be cooked outdoors or for a short time inside.

storing meat

All fresh meat should be loosely wrapped and stored in the coldest part of the refrigerator (35° to 40°), at all times except when cooking, serving or eating. The same is true of cured meat, except that it should be tightly wrapped. No meat should be allowed to stand at room temperature for longer than 3 hours without being heated to at least 140°. This time is cumulative, which means that time out of the refrigerator and oven add up even though the meat is refrigerated in between. Be careful about packing meat sandwiches in lunches, unless the sandwiches are frozen first. Frozen sandwiches insulated in lunch boxes don't usually thaw for a couple of hours.

freezing meat

Moisture loss and rancidity are the two main problems as far as freezing of meats is concerned. The proper use of strong, moisture proof, vapor proof, pliable paper will solve both of these problems. Be sure that any sharp bones are wrapped with extra foil or they will poke right through the paper. That is hard on both the meat and the disposition. Label and date all packages going into the freezer. Use them in rotation and during the recommended storage period.

Product	Freezer storage period 0°
Fresh raw pork	3 to 4 months
Chops	4 to 8 months
Roasts	1 month
Sausage	3 to 4 months
Variety meats	2 weeks
Cured or processed pork	2 to 3 months
Frankfurts	2 to 3 months
Ham	2 to 3 months
Cooked pork	
Cooked pork and pork dishes	
Gravy and meat broth	

thawing meat

Meats may be thawed a number of ways depending upon your time and facilities. For instance, meats may be thawed in the refrigerator in 24 hours to 4 days according to the size of the meat. It may be thawed under cold running water while still in airtight wrapping. Frozen meat can also be thawed in its original wrapper at room temperatures of 60° to 72° away from heat. Microwave ovens can also thaw frozen products in an unbelievably short time. Manufacturers instructions should be followed. Whatever method you use, *be sure* to *cook* or *refrigerate* the meat as soon as it has thawed.

cooking frozen meats

Meats can be cooked from the frozen state but two things must be taken into consideration:

1. Most cuts will take up to 50% longer to cook.

2. Smaller cuts, like chops or steaks, sometimes cook before they brown and some roasts get too brown before cooking to the well done stage.

If the emergency isn't too great, it is easier to thaw the meat first.

fresh pork roasts

Delicious roast pork, crispy brown outside, tender, white and juicy inside, is one of the great joys of the dinner table. It is easy to prepare and relatively economical, so naturally homemakers like pork. Serve cold or hot and vary the seasonings so the family won't tire of it.

LEG

Same shape and size as ham

SIRLOIN ROAST

Hip and back bone difficult to carve

CENTER CUT LOIN

T-bone—tenderloin. Choicest quality. Easiest to carve.

BLADE BONE LOIN

Flat blade bone

CROWN ROAST

Two rib sections tied together to form a crown.

PICNIC SHOULDER

Same shape but smaller than leg.

CUSHION

Boned but not rolled picnic. Good value in cost per serving.

BOSTON BUTT

Square shoulder cut. Blade bone in. Not very difficult to carve.

SELECTION: Remember to look for pale pink color and fine texture. Be sure to consider the cost per serving. Allow for bone.

continued on next page

Buying

Amount to buy:

Approximate Size:	Yield:
Leg, bone-in (12-16 lbs.)*	2-3 servings per pound
Leg, boned—rolled (10-14 lbs.)*	4 servings per pound
Loin center cut (4-7 lbs.)	2-3 servings per pound
Sirloin roast (3-4 lbs.)	2-3 servings per pound
Blade bone loin roast (3-5 lbs.)	1-2 servings per pound
Cushion (boneless) (3-5 lbs.)	4 servings per pound
Boston butt (3-8 lbs.)	2-3 servings per pound
Boneless Boston butt (2-4 lbs.)	4 servings per pound
Picnic, bone-in or rolled (4-10 lbs.)	2 to 4 servings per pound
Crown roast (3-10 lbs.)	2 ribs per serving

*May be cut into smaller roasts

Loin Roasts—Be sure to ask the meat dealer to cut the back bone loose from the ribs and the rest of the bones. Roast the meat on the back bone but remove it before taking it to the table.

Crown Roast—Have the backbone removed completely before it is tied.

Storing

Be sure to take the meat right home and refrigerate it immediately, loosely wrapped in the coldest part of your refrigerator. If you plan to keep it longer than three or four days, it would be better to freeze it. Flavor is a fleeting thing and departs more every hour before it is frozen or eaten. After the meat has been cooked, make sure that it doesn't stand at room temperature for longer than three hours. The danger zone for meat is 40° to 140°. For further information, see page 12.

Freezing

Roasts may be held in a freezer at 0°temperature, if properly wrapped, for 4-8 months.

Thawing

See page 13.

roasting

1. Preheat the oven to 325°. Place meat fat side up on rack in a shallow roasting pan. If desired, season with salt or seasoned salt, pepper, thyme or rosemary. Slivers of garlic may be placed in gashes in fat for extra flavor.

2. Place meat thermometer in center of meat. Take care not to let the bulb touch bone or fat. Note on using a meat thermometer: As meat cooks, it contracts and often dislodges thermometer. Before taking final reading, push thermometer down about a quarter of an inch.

3. Do not cover pan. A half cup water in the bottom of the pan keeps the drippings from burning and makes better gravy. Lining the pan with foil makes cleaning very easy.

4. Cook all pork roasts until the center registers 170° and until there are no pink juices running out of the meat when pierced with fork.

timetable for roasting fresh pork

CUT	AVERAGE WEIGHT (POUNDS)	OVEN TEMPERATURE CONSTANT	INTERIOR TEMPERATURE WHEN REMOVED FROM OVEN	APPROXIMATE COOKING TIME (MINUTES PER POUND)
Loin				
Center	3-5	325°	170°	30-35
Half	5-7	325°	170°	35-40
Blade loin or sirloin	3-4	325°	170°	40-45
Rolled	3-5	325°	170°	35-45
Crown Roast (no filling)	4-6	325°	170°	35-40
Picnic Shoulder	5-8	325°	170°	30-35
Rolled	3-5	325°	170°	35-40
Cushion style	3-5	325°	170°	30-35
Boston Shoulder	4-6	325°	170°	40-45
Leg (Fresh Ham)				
Whole (bone in)	12-16	325°	170°	22-26
Whole	10-14	325°	170°	24-28
Half (bone in)	5-8	325°	170°	35-40

gravy

1-1/2 tablespoons
  drippings
1 tablespoon flour
1 cup water or milk
  or half of each

Blend drippings and flour over low heat. Slowly add liquid. Stir and heat to boiling. Boil 5 minutes. Season with salt and pepper to taste. Yield: 1 cup.

HINTS: If the color doesn't suit you, stir in a little kitchen bouquet. About 1/4 teaspoon onion juice per cup of gravy gives it a delicious flavor.

CHEFS TRICK: Brown dry flour in a heavy skillet over low heat. Stir constantly until the flour becomes a rich brown. Use about a third more brown flour than white for thickening. Extra brown flour can be stored at room temperature for future use.

apricot glaze for roast pork

1 can (12 oz.) apricot
  nectar
1 teaspoon dry hot
  mustard
2 teaspoons soy sauce
1 tablespoon sugar
1/2 teaspoon
  seasoned salt
1 pork roast

Boil nectar to one half the volume. Combine with other ingredients. Let stand at least two hours before using. Baste roast with glaze during the last 40 minutes of cooking in a 325° oven. Roast is finished when meat thermometer in the center of the meat reads 170°, no pink can be seen in the center of the meat and it is tender. See page 17 for approximate cooking times. Pass the remainder of the warm glaze with the roast. Yield: scant 2/3 cup.

MENU: Apricot Glazed Roast Pork, Baked Potatoes, Broccoli, Hollandaise Sauce, Tossed Green Salad, Green Apple Pie, Cheddar Cheese, Coffee or Milk.

GARNISH: Celery leaves and baked potatoes on platter around roast.

BUSY DAY TIP: This sauce can be made one or two days ahead and stored, covered, in the refrigerator.

roast pork a l'orange

2 tablespoons butter
    or margarine
1 cup orange juice
1/2 cup dry white wine
3 tablespoons
    brown sugar
1/4 teaspoon orange
    peel, grated
3/4 teaspoon
    seasoned salt
1/8 teaspoon
    dry mustard
Dash white pepper
1/4 teaspoon
    ground thyme
1 teaspoon cornstarch
1 pork roast

Combine and heat all ingredients except cornstarch until butter melts. Roast in 325° oven and baste every half hour. Use time table and instructions on page 17. When roast is finished (170° on meat thermometer), mix cornstarch with a little water. Add to sauce and heat and stir until thickened and clear. Yield: 2 cups.

MENU: Roast Pork a l'Orange, Mashed Sweet Potatoes, Dilled Green Beans, Perfection Salad, Marble Cake a la Mode, Tea or Milk.

GARNISH: Mound mashed sweet potatoes on half inch slices of oranges. Brush with butter. Place in oven the last half hour that the roast is cooking. Place on platter with roast.

roast pork with cherry sauce

1 can (16 oz.) sour
    cherry pie filling
1/4 cup lemon juice
1 tablespoon brown
    sugar
1/4 cup dark rum
    (optional)
1/4 teaspoon
    seasoned salt
2 dashes white pepper
1/2 teaspoon ginger
1 pork roast

Heat all ingredients to boiling. Simmer and stir a few minutes. Serve hot with roast pork. See page 17 for method and time of cooking. Yield: about 2 cups.

MENU: Roast Pork with Cherry Sauce, Buttered Brown Rice, Mixed Vegetables, Tomato and Guacamole Salad, Chocolate Floating Island, Lady Fingers, Coffee, Milk

GARNISH: Twisted lemon slices on parsley. (Use the ends of the lemon squeezed for lemon juice.)

sauerkraut stuffed cushion shoulder of pork

1 boneless pork
  shoulder cushion
Salt, pepper, poultry
  seasoning
2 cups finely chopped
  sauerkraut

Sprinkle the inside of boneless shoulder with salt, pepper, and poultry seasoning. Stuff with sauerkraut. Be sure to stuff the meat full enough to make the roast look nice and full. Skewer the roast shut. Place on rack in roasting pan. Roast in 325° oven for 30 to 35 minutes per pound or until the roast meat thermometer stuck in the center of the meat reads 170°. Yield: 4 to 6 servings, about 8 oz. each.

MENU: Sauerkraut Stuffed Cushion Shoulder of Pork, Oven Browned Potatoes, Glazed Whole Small Carrots, Spring Salad, Peach Pie, Coffee, Milk.

GARNISH: Oven Browned Potatoes, Glazed Whole Carrots. Celery Leaves or Parsley.

prune stuffed cushion of pork

1 package herb
  stuffing (7 oz.)
15 finely chopped
  prunes—not cooked
1 cushion style pork
  shoulder roast
  (3-5 lb.)

Prepare stuffing according to package directions but make it a little on the dry side. Mix in prunes. Stuff meat with enough to make the roast plump and round. Skewer and lace or sew meat closed. Roast in a preheated 325° oven for 30 to 35 minutes per pound or until meat thermometer reads 170°. Yield: 4 to 6 servings about 8 oz. each.

NOTE: Bake remainder of stuffing during the last 30 minutes. If roast isn't brown enough, put it under the broiler for a few minutes. This is a trick of the chefs.

MENU: Prune Stuffed Cushion Pork Shoulder Roast, Corn Souffle Casserole, Buttered Baby Beets, Three Bean Salad, Spice Cake, Coffee, Milk.

GARNISH: Spiced Crab Apples on Grape Leaves.

HINT: Be sure to ask your meat man to note the weight of the cushion roast on the package. You will then be able to estimate the cooking time.

crown roast of pork

This is made of two rib sections shaped and tied into a circle with the ribs on the outside and the meat on the inside. They usually contain 12 to 26 ribs. Crown Roast is the fancy party meat that is so simple for anyone to cook and carve. The meat man really does the work. NOTE: Don't forget to make sure that *all* of the backbone has been removed so that carving will be a matter of slicing between every rib.

Preparing for the oven: Wrap the rib ends with foil to keep them from burning and turning black. Don't cook with ground meat in the center because it will take too long for the roast to cook and the meat might be dry. If desired, cook the ground meat in a skillet and combine with a bread dressing which can be cooked 30 or 40 minutes before the roast is ready to come out of the oven.

Cooking the roast: Place the meat on a rack in a shallow pan. Roast in a 325° oven. Roast 35 to 40 minutes per pound for meat that is thoroughly thawed but is at refrigerator temperature. A roast meat thermometer will register 170° when placed in the center of the meat.

Serving: Plan on one or two ribs per serving. Of course you will have to estimate how many servings your guests will want.

Garnishing: When the roast is finished, garnish the bones with white paper frills, gay red cherry tomatoes, bright green brussels sprouts or use your own imagination to see what you can dream up. Serve the roast on a round chop plate. For the sake of your china, silver, and carving set, be sure to use a wooden insert on the chop plate. If you don't have one and can't find one in the stores, draw a pattern of the inside of the chop plate. Take it to the nearest lumber yard and they will probably cut one out of hard wood for you. Use watercress or parsley around the roast.

MENU: Crown Roast of Pork, Bread Dressing, Cherry Tomato Garnish, Buttered Asparagus, Cold Sherry Apple and Celery Salad*, Caramel Flan, Coffee, Milk.

*Sherry Apple and Celery Salad: Core, peel and quarter tart apples. Poach apples in a syrup made of 1/2 cup cinnamon candies, 2 cups water, and 2/3 cup sherry wine, until tender. Chill. Make a salad of apples, celery, marshmallows and mayonnaise.

NOTE: This is a beautiful salad for any red holiday like Christmas, Valentine's Day or Washington's Birthday.

pork tenderloin

This is the most tender and the most expensive cut of pork.

Selecting: The tenderloin of pork is generally 9 to 12 inches long and weighs 3/4 to 1-1/2 pounds each. The ends are tapered and the centers are round.

Buying: Pork tenderloins are available fresh or frozen, whole, half or sliced and pounded into thin patties. This pounding method is called frenching.

Storing: If the tenderloins are frozen and you don't plan to use them for a while, rewrap them properly in foil or freezer paper. Be sure to label them with the name and date. Use them within three or four months for best quality. Fresh tenderloins should be loosely wrapped and stored in the coldest part of the refrigerator. Plan to use them within 2 or 3 days or freeze the meat as noted above.

Cooking Whole
Whole roasted pork tenderloins are best when completely thawed before cooking. They may be marinated in your favorite salad dressing (oil and vinegar or lemon juice and seasonings), or marinade. Tuck the thin ends of the tenderloins under before roasting. If the meat is quite lean, skewer a slice of bacon on each tenderloin. Roast in a 325° oven for 30 to 50 minutes or until the center of the meat registers 170°.

Serving: Cut the meat on the diagonal to make the slices a little larger and more attractive.

Garnishing: Fresh thyme, marjoram or mint leaves are all very pretty around this small but delicious roast. If you really want to splurge, add a few preserved kumquats. Heavenly!!

MENU: Roast Pork Tenderloin, Buttered Mashed Hominy, Sauteed Cherry Tomatoes and Green Onions, Sunshine Salad, Gingerbread, Coffee, Milk.

NOTE: Have you ever tried putting nuts and raisins in gingerbread? Aren't they tasty?

carving

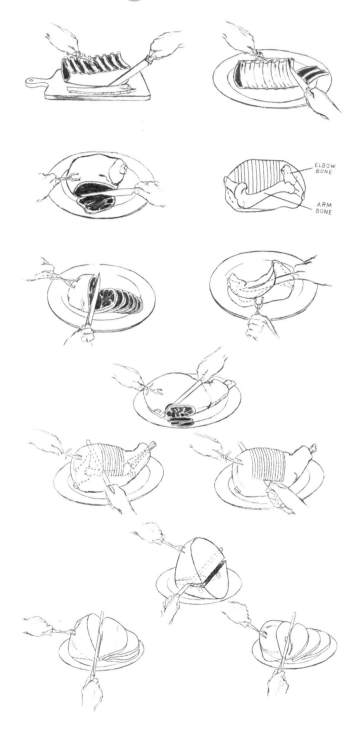

Pork Loin

Before roast is brought to table remove back bone leaving as little meat on it as possible. Place roast on platter with rib side facing carver so he can see angle of ribs and can make his slices accordingly.

Insert fork in top of roast. Make slices by cutting closely along each side of rib bone. One slice will contain the rib; the next will be boneless.

Picnic shoulder

Carving is the same for both a roasted (baked) smoked picnic and a roasted (baked) fresh picnic. Remove lengthwise slice as shown here. Turn picnic so that it rests on surface just cut.

Cut down to arm bone at a point near elbow bone. Turn knife and cut along arm bone to remove boneless arm meat.

Carve boneless arm meat by making perpendicular slices from top of meat down to cutting board.

Remove meat from each side of arm bone. Carve the two boneless pieces.

Whole ham

Ham is placed on platter with decorated or fat side up and shank to carver's right. Location of bones in right and left hams may be confusing so double check location of knee cap which may be on near or far side of ham. Remove two or three lengthwise slices from thin side of ham which contains knee cap.

Make perpendicular slices down to leg bone or lift off boneless cushion similar to method illustrated for picnic shoulder.

Release slices by cutting along leg bone.

Shank half of ham

With shank at carver's left, turn ham so thick cushion side is up. Cut along top of leg and shank bones and under fork to lift off boneless cushion.

Place cushion meat on carving board and make perpendicular slices as illustrated.

Cut around leg bone with tip of knife to remove meat from this bone. Turn meat so that thickest side is down. Slice in same manner as cushion piece.

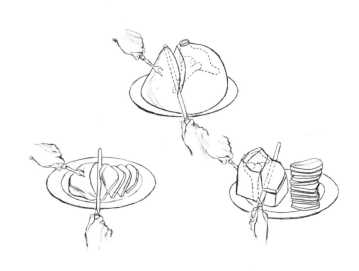

Butt half of ham

Place butt half of ham on platter with face or center on carving board. Cut down along aitch bone to remove boneless piece from side of ham. The boneless piece may be on either near or far side depending on whether it is from right or left leg.

With boneless piece resting on freshly cut surface, carve it into desirable cross-grain servings.

Hold remaining piece with fork and carve across meat until knife strikes aitch bone. Release each slice from bone with tip of knife and lift it to side of platter.

Center leg roasts

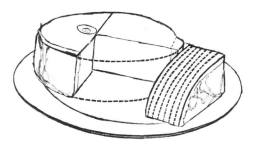

Center leg roasts of pork and thick center ham slices should be divided into thirds. Turn one section at a time on its side so that it can be carved across the grain. The leg bone must be removed from the end section before carving. Sometimes it will be easier to carve the meat around the bone as two separate pieces rather than as one piece. When carving relatively small boneless pieces of meat, it is frequently advantageous to use the carver's helper. Put tines into meat so they are parallel to face of meat and perpendicular to carving board. Remove slices until tines are reached, then start at back side of meat and carve up to tines. The last slice will be held in the tines and the entire piece will have been carved without removing the fork.

Crown roasts

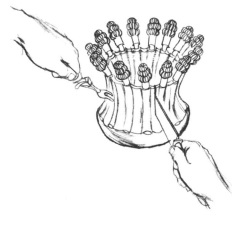

Crown roasts of pork may be garnished so elaborately that at first glance they may appear difficult to carve, but such is not the case. Remove from the center of the crown any garnish that might interfere with carving. Slice down between the ribs removing one rib chop at a time. Stuffing in the center of the crown, depending upon its consistency, may be either carved or removed with a spoon and served with the meat. The usual crown roast contains about 14 ribs, but crowns with 40 or 50 ribs can be made. To facilitate carving and serving, the back bone should be completely removed in the market.

fresh pork chops and steaks

The shape of the bone in steaks and chops is the key. Since nearly all cuts are tender and most can be interchanged in recipes, make your choice according to the price and size. Usually the loin and the butterfly are the most expensive. The loin has the tenderloin which is the choicest and most tender cut of all. The butterfly is a boned double rib chop that has been cut almost in two toward the rib side. It is then flattened to form a chop that is twice the size of a regular chop. This is considered by some to be the most elegant of all chops.

Selecting

Look for pale pink, fine textured and well marbled meat for best flavor. Marbling is specks of fat distributed throughout the meat. Be sure to count the cost per serving rather than the cost per pound of meat.

Buying

This will depend upon the size of the animal and, most important, on the thickness of the chop or steak. In general, chops and steaks shouldn't be less than 1/2 inch thick for best flavor and texture. Thicker chops and steaks are even better.

Sirloin	1/2 inch	6 to 8 oz.
Loin	1 inch	5 to 6 oz.
Rib	1 inch	4 to 5 oz.
Butterfly	1 inch	7 to 9 oz.
Blade	1/2 inch	6 to 8 oz.
Arm	1/2 inch	6 to 8 oz.

Fortunately in this day and age, precut and packaged chops can be counted when you make your selection. The above list will give you an idea of the number of chops per pound.

How many to buy: You are the only one who knows how much the individual members of your family will eat. Recipes are written for average appetites. If father eats two, teen age son eats three, six-year-old Susie eats a half a chop and you eat one, you'll know how many to buy and prepare. Budgets are handled as much by avoiding waste as by initial economy.

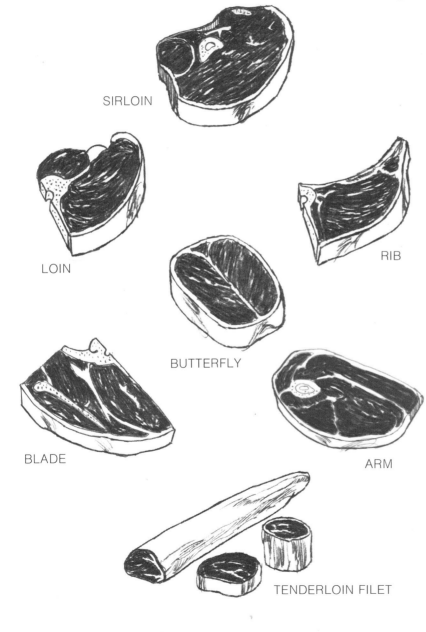

SIRLOIN

LOIN

RIB

BUTTERFLY

BLADE

ARM

TENDERLOIN FILET

Storing

Both the packer and the retailer have tried hard to get meat to you in prime condition. It's your responsibility to keep up the good work. Be sure to refrigerate the pork as soon as possible. Unless the meat package states otherwise, remove the market wrapping and cover it loosely. If you plan to keep it longer than three days, freeze the meat. If there are leftovers, cover them and store in the refrigerator as soon as the table is cleared. Don't forget them! Check in the leftover section for ideas.

Freezing

Wrap the chops in meal size portions. However, just in case a few have to be added or subtracted at the last minute, put two pieces of wax paper between each chop. Use your favorite freezer paper and wrap according to instructions. In case there aren't any instructions, use the drugstore wrap and make sure that as much air as possible is forced out of the package. Bind with freezer tape and mark with a grease pencil, the date, the product and the amount of product. It's maddening to thaw the wrong product or the wrong amount of product! Plan to use chops within 3 to 4 months after freezing. If held longer, the fat might turn rancid and develop an off-flavor.

Thawing

Meat may be thawed in three ways depending on the amount of time you have and your preference. The thawing time will depend on the amount of meat as well as the method that you use.

1. Put the meat in the refrigerator. Leave the freezer wrapping on it. Four average servings should thaw in 12 hours.

2. Put the meat, with the wrapper on it, on a rack and thaw it at room temperature. Thawing time will depend on room temperature as well as on the amount of meat. Caution!! Refrigerate or cook the chops as soon as they are thawed.

3. This is the quickest. Place the wrapped meat in a pan of cold water or thaw the meat under running cold water. Be sure that the paper doesn't have a hole in it or you'll lose some of the good pork flavor.

Braising *for rich and tender chops and steaks*

Pork tastes best when it is cooked until no pink shows but it is still juicy. Chops and steaks are delightful when cooked in moist heat, as in braising. The liquid may be its own juice, fruit juice, bouillon or a mixture. In general, remove extra fat that may be on the chops. Dust them in flour that has been seasoned with salt and pepper. Brown the chops in hot fat. Pour off the fat, add liquid

continued on next page

to about half the thickness of the chop and cover. Cook slowly over low heat on the surface of the range or in a 350° oven. The time will depend on the thickness of the chop and will vary from 25 minutes for those a half inch thick to 2 hours for the elegant inch and a half masterpieces. Just be sure there is no trace of pink in the center and the meat is fork tender. For other recipes, see the later pages in this section and in barbecue on pages 52 and 53.

MENU: Braised Pork Chops, Mashed Potatoes, Pennsylvania Dutch Spinach, Carrot and Raisin Salad, Baked Apples, Coffee, Milk.

Broiling

As with other kinds of meat, pork—both fresh and smoked— should be at least 3/4 or 1 inch thick to be tasty when broiled. Slash outside fat every inch to keep the chop from curling. Use the manufacturer's instructions for broiling in your range. In general, the broiler should be preheated and the broiler pan should be 2 to 4 inches from the source of heat. Fresh pork should be broiled 20 to 25 minutes total time. Ham should be broiled 10 to 20 minutes total time. Broil the meat half the time on each side. Since each piece of meat will require a different time, check about 2 minutes before the time is up. To check, cut along the bone and look for pinkness. In the case of ham, check to be sure the texture is right and the meat is thoroughly hot. *Hint:* If you line the broiler pan with foil before using, it will be easier to clean.

MENU: Broiled Pork Chops, Broiled Tomatoes, Potatoes au Gratin, Cabbage Slaw, Gingerbread, Tea, Milk.

Seasoning tricks

Pork and chicken have a lot in common when it comes to seasoning. Citrus fruits, tart apples or cherries are all go-togethers as far as fresh pork is concerned. Herb combinations like poultry seasoning, herb salts, or any used alone are tasty. Sage, thyme, rosemary, marjoram, prepared mustard and tarragon are all seasonings that our friends have liked. Just remember, use discretion with herbs. It is better to use a little more the next time than to get too much in the first time. A good rule of thumb with the dried herbs is to use 1/4 teaspoon per four servings as a starter. Try different kinds of prepared mustard. Dijon, Dusseldorf and horseradish are a few that you will find at your supermarket. Add these to the braising liquid or coat the top of the chops after browning.

Garnishes

Greens—parsley, mint, or celery leaves are pretty and easy to use to garnish platters of meat. Pickled or preserved fruits are colorful and very tasty with pork. Kumquats, peaches, apples, and pears are good examples. If the party is especially elegant, you might use yours or Aunt Hatty's prize watermelon pickles.

pork chop roast

6-12 pork chops
  1 inch thick
Salt
White pepper
Poultry seasoning

Sprinkle surfaces of chops with seasoning. Stand chops up together, fat side up. Skewer them from each end to the center so that the chops form a roast. Place in a shallow roasting pan in a preheated 325° oven. Roast 30 to 35 minutes per pound until a roast meat thermometer registers 170°. Remove skewers before serving. Yield: 1-2 chops/serving—6 to 12 chops total.

MENU: Pork Chop Roast, Sweet Potato Balls, Minted Peas, Crisp Garden Salad—Green Goddess Dressing, Lemon Refrigerator Pudding, Tea, Milk.

GARNISH: Serve roast on platter with sweet potato balls garnished with whole spiced crab apples on leaves of mustard greens (uncooked).

sweet sour pork chops

4-6 pork chops
Flour, seasoned to
  taste
1/2 cup cider vinegar
1/4 cup granulated
  sugar
1/4 cup light brown
  sugar, firmly packed
2 tablespoons
  soy sauce
1/8 teaspoon salt
1/4 cup chopped
  green onions, green
  tops too
1 green pepper,
  coarsely chopped
1 cup coarsely
  shredded carrots

Dust chops with flour. Brown chops in drippings. Drain any excess fat. Combine and cook vinegar, sugars, soy and salt to a thin syrup. Add onions and green pepper. Pour sauce over chops. Cover and cook slowly for 1 hour or until tender. Add carrots. Stir just until hot. Serve chops with the sauce that clings. Pass extra hot sauce. Yield: 4 servings, about 1-1/4 cups sauce.

MENU: Sweet Sour Pork Chops, Rice, Brussels Sprouts, Sliced Tomato and Artichoke Hearts, Devils Food Cake, Coffee, Milk.

GARNISH: Serve chops on rice with greens.

pork chops in spanish sauce

This is for the young brides who want to cook pork chops like Mother—his or hers.

2 tablespoons flour
1/4 teaspoon seasoned salt
Dash black pepper
4 loin pork chops— 1 inch thick
1/2 cup water

Combine flour, salt and pepper. Dust on pork. Brown chops slowly in pork fat or butter. Transfer to baking dish. Add water and cover. Bake 10 minutes in a preheated 350° oven.

Spanish Sauce
2 tablespoons butter
1/2 cup chopped green onions
1/2 cup chopped celery
1/4 cup chopped green pepper
1 can (16 oz.) tomatoes
1 teaspoon seasoned salt
1/4 teaspoon pepper
3 dashes Tabasco Sauce

Melt butter. Cook onions, celery and green pepper until wilted. Don't brown. Add tomatoes and seasonings. Cover and cook 10 minutes. Pour over chops. Cook 1-1/2 hours or until chops are fork tender. Yield: 4 servings.

NOTE: This recipe can be increased or decreased as desired. If your guests are late—be calm! Just turn the oven to very low. Add more water or juice if the sauce cooks away.

ALTERNATE CUTS: Any cut of chops will work fine. That's the beauty of cooking pork chops. If you want them thinner, just cook the number your family needs. Decrease the cooking time. See basic preparation on page 30.

MENU: Pork Chops in Spanish Sauce, Rice, Green Beans and Mushrooms, Molded Avocado Lemon Salad*, Spice Cake, Tea, Milk.

GARNISH: Serve Pork Chops on a bed of rice with Spanish Sauce over all. It's picture pretty.

*Avocado Lemon Salad is simply avocado that has been mashed and seasoned with a little horseradish, onion or Tabasco Sauce and folded into lemon gelatin.

chex 'n chops

3 cups Corn Chex
3/4 cup drained whole kernel corn
1/3 cup coarsely chopped onion
1 teaspoon salt
3 dashes Tabasco Sauce
1/4 teaspoon rosemary, finely crushed
1/4 teaspoon dried parsley or chervil
6 pork chops—1 inch thick, for stuffing

Butter shallow baking dish and preheat oven to 350° Combine Corn Chex, corn, onion, salt, Tabasco, rosemary and parsley. Stuff pork chops with corn mixture. Bake 1 hour and 15 minutes or until tender and brown. Yield: 6 servings.

MENU: Chex 'N Chops, Buttered Broccoli, Baked Potatoes, Pineapple Lime Molded Salad, Butterscotch Sundaes with Salted Peanuts or Pecans, Coffee, Milk.

GARNISH: Serve the chops on a platter and group bright red and yellow sweet pickled peppers on parsley or celery leaves at several spots around the platter.

pork chops senegalese

(a mild flavored curry sauce)

6 pork chops, any thickness desired
Seasoned flour for dusting
1 can (13 oz.) Senegalese Soup

Dust pork chops. Brown in bacon drippings or pork fat. Place in baking dish. Pour on soup. Cover. Bake in a 350° oven for 1 hour or until fork tender. Thicken soup with flour or cornstarch. Pass sauce with chops. Yield: 3-4 servings.

MENU: Pork Chops Senegalese, Rice Pilaf, Baked Tomatoes, Waldorf Salad, Toffee and Whipped Cream Filled Angel Cake, Coffee, Milk.

GARNISH: Serve chops on pilaf and garnish with baked tomatoes and mint leaves.

pork chops with orange rice

2 tablespoons flour
1/4 teaspoon seasoned salt
Dash black pepper
4 rib pork chops — 1 inch thick
2 tablespoons butter or margarine
1/2 cup water

Combine flour and seasonings. Dust on pork chops. Brown chops on both sides in butter or drippings. Add water and cover. Cook slowly for 20 minutes.

Orange Rice

2/3 cup rice
1/2 cup orange juice
1 cup chicken bouillon
1/4 teaspoon ginger
1/4 teaspoon dry mustard

Preheat oven to 350°. Combine all ingredients. Place in shallow 2-quart casserole. Cover with foil and bake 20 minutes. Put chops on rice. Cover again and bake 40 minutes or until the chops are fork tender. Yield: 4 servings.

MENU: Pork Chops with Orange Rice, Asparagus Amandine, Buttered Carrots, Perfection Salad, Coconut Pie, Coffee, Milk.

GARNISH: Thin orange slices that were cut off before the oranges were squeezed. Make one cut to the center and twist the ends in the opposite direction. Use parsley with the twists.

creamy mushroomed pork chops

This is a pretty dish that can be increased for a party.

4 pork chops, 1 inch thick
Seasoned flour for dusting
2 tablespoons butter
1/2 pound fresh mushrooms
2 tablespoons finely chopped onion
1 cup sour cream
2 tablespoons flour
1 cup chicken bouillon
3 dashes white pepper
1/4 teaspoon ground marjoram
2 cups cooked green noodles
1/4 cup grated parmesan cheese
2 tablespoons chopped ripe olives

Preheat oven to 350°. Dust chops and brown. Slice mushrooms and saute them quickly in butter with onions. Stir flour into sour cream. Stir and heat just to boiling. Slowly stir in bouillon. Heat to boiling.

Add seasonings, cheese and olives. Mix with noodles. Pour into a shallow casserole. Top with chops. Bake covered for 1 hour. Uncover and bake another 30 minutes or until tender. Yield: 4 servings. NOTE: If you can't find green noodles use the plain but add a tablespoon or two of tomato sauce for color.

MENU: Creamy Mushroomed Pork Chops, Buttered Carrots, Cinnamon Apple Slices, Sunshine Salad, Cold Chocolate Souffle, Coffee, Milk.

GARNISH: Parsley and a cherry tomato on top.

ribs and back bones

Back Ribs—braise—cook in liquid
Country Style Back Bones—cook in liquid
Spareribs—braise—roast—barbecue

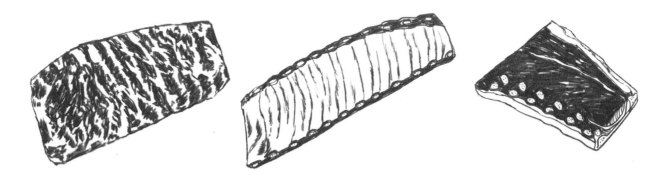

SPARERIBS
The smaller the bones
and the more meat,
the more expensive.

BACK RIBS
These are less
expensive and
less tender.

COUNTRY STYLE BACK BONES
These are strictly
moist heat, long
cookery cuts.

Buying

Amount to buy Approximate size	Yield
Spareribs 2-3 lbs.	2-3 servings
Back ribs 2-3 lbs.	2-3 servings
Country Style Back Bones 2-4 lbs.	1-2 servings

Be sure to ask the meat man to cut between the bones at the large end.

Sometimes, especially in the South, ribs are cured. Instead of being pink and white, they are gray. Be sure to check because cured ribs must be soaked in water or simmered in water before cooking to remove some of the salt.

Storing
Wrap the meat loosely in waxed paper and store in the coldest part of the refrigerator. Cook within 3-5 days.

continued on next page

ribs and back bones continued

Freezing

Wrap the ribs in heavy foil or freezer paper. Seal with freezer tape and label and date. Thaw and cook within 3 to 4 months.

Thawing

Since ribs have so little meat, they thaw very quickly. If they are being braised, they can be thawed quickly in the oven.

Braising

Cut the ribs or back bones into pieces that are convenient to manage. Brown them quickly in hot fat. Place over sauerkraut with 1/2 cup hot water or in your favorite barbecue sauce. Cover. Cook slowly for 1 to 2 hours until the meat is thoroughly cooked and is not pink next to the bone. These can be done in a pressure cooker. Follow manufacturer's instructions.

Alternate: Some people prefer to cut a large onion and put on ribs. They substitute chicken or beef bouillon for barbecue sauce. After ribs are cooked, thicken liquid and serve over potatoes or rice. This is especially good for country style back bones.

Moist heat cookery

This is the same as braising except more liquid is used. Be sure that the liquid is kept to simmering to prevent toughening or excessive shrinkage. Add vegetables during the last 30 minutes. Mighty tasty!

ribs and succotash

1 package (10-1/2 oz.) frozen whole kernel corn
1 package (10-1/2 oz.) frozen lima beans
1-1/2 to 2 slabs of ribs (enough for 4)
2 tablespoons Worcestershire sauce

Cook corn and beans according to label instructions. Cut ribs into 4 pieces. Brush on both sides with Worcestershire sauce. Place over combined and seasoned vegetables. Add 1/2 cup hot water. Cover. Roast in a 350° oven for 1 hour or until ribs are tender and not pink next to the bone.

MENU: Ribs and Succotash, Baked Potatoes, Carrot and Raisin Salad, Hot Cherry Pie, Coffee, Milk.

GARNISH: Spiced crab apples, celery leaves.

sweet and sour spareribs

(appetizers)

1 pound meaty spareribs, chopped into 2-inch pieces
1 tablespoon soy sauce
1 tablespoon water

Brush ribs with soy-water combination. Bake in a 350° oven about an hour or until brown, crisp and tender. Stir once or twice during cooking time.

Sweet-Sour Sauce

1/2 cup brown sugar, firmly packed
1/2 cup vinegar
1/4 cup sherry
1-1/2 teaspoons soy sauce
1/2 teaspoon hot dry mustard
1-1/2 teaspoons cornstarch
2 tablespoons water
1/8 teaspoon powdered ginger

Combine sugar, vinegar, sherry, soy and dry mustard. Heat to boiling. Combine cornstarch and water. Add to sugar mixture. Stir and heat until thickened. Stir in ginger. Pour over spareribs and serve OR refrigerate or freeze. Reheat before serving. Yield: about 20 pieces, depending on size of ribs. NOTE: This is just as good when served as the main dish.

MENU: Sweet and Sour Spareribs, Mixed Vegetables, Parsley Potatoes, Tomato Aspic, Spice Cake a la Mode, Coffee, Milk.

GARNISH: Preserved kumquats.

curried pork and apples

Leftover pork
2 cups diced cooked pork
1/4 cup butter
3 tablespoons flour
2 cups chicken bouillon
1 teaspoon curry powder
1/2 cup finely chopped tart apple

Brown pork slightly in butter. Sprinkle with flour. Mix bouillon and curry powder. Slowly stir bouillon into pork. Stir and heat to boiling. Lower heat. Stir in apple. Cover. Heat 20 minutes until apples are cooked. Serve on rice. Yield: 4 servings.

MENU: Curried Apples and Pork, Fluffy Rice, Julienne Carrots, Crisp Green Salad with Peanut French Dressing, Chilled Melon, Coffee, Milk.

GARNISH: Watercress

casseroles

Impromptu (Cooked diced pork — leftover)

2 tablespoons butter
1/2 pound pork sausage
2 cups chopped cooked pork
2 cups croutons
2 tablespoons chopped parsley
2 tablespoons chopped chives
1/2 teaspoon crushed dried marjoram
1/2 teaspoon grated lemon peel
1 can (10-1/2 oz.) cream of mushroom soup

Cook and crumble pork sausage. Add pork and brown slightly. Stir in croutons. If there is excess fat, drain. If not, add other ingredients. Cover. Cook over low heat for 25 to 30 minutes. Sprinkle additional chopped parsley over top just before serving. Yield: 4 servings.

MENU: Impromptu, Mashed Sweet Potatoes, Buttered Green Beans, Celery Cabbage Salad, Peppermint Ice Cream with Chocolate Sauce, Coffee, Milk.

Pork Tenderloin Casserole

2 pork tenderloins
Flour
Butter or bacon drippings
1 cup chicken bouillon
1 cup dry white wine
1/4 to 1/2 teaspoon ground thyme
1/2 teaspoon kitchen bouquet
1 teaspoon onion juice
2 cans (4 oz.) or 1/2 lb. fresh mushrooms

Cut pork into bite size pieces. Coat in flour. Brown in butter. (Some like to use a skillet and transfer meat to four individual casseroles.) Saute sliced mushrooms quickly. Add the other ingredients to the mushrooms and meat. Heat to boiling. Cover and place in a preheated 350° oven or transfer to casseroles and cook in the oven for 30 minutes. Remove cover and cook for another 30 minutes to thicken sauce slightly. Yield: 4 servings.

MENU: Pork Tenderloin Casserole, Curried Rice, Buttered Broccoli, Tomato Aspic, Warm Plum Lattice Pie a la mode, Coffee, Milk.

GARNISH: Serve on rice with chopped parsley on top.

NOTE: If you think you don't like curry, try just a little — I'll bet you'll like it. Mild curry is really too good and too pretty to miss.

Party Pork Casserole

This takes quite a while to make but it tastes so good that it is well worth the time. Make it some morning when you have to be home anyway and store it in the freezer.

1 pound fresh mushrooms
2 cups chicken bouillon
1 cup chopped onions
3 tablespoons plus 1/2 cup butter
2 cups cubed, cooked lean pork
2 cups (10 oz.) tiny cooked shrimp
8 oz. green or white noodles, cooked
1 can (16 oz.) tomatoes
1 cup sliced ripe olives
1 cup finely chopped parsley
1/3 cup flour
1-1/2 cups milk
2 packages (3 oz. each) cream cheese
1 teaspoon salt
1/4 teaspoon white pepper
1/4 teaspoon ground thyme
1/4 teaspoon ground basil
2 cups shredded cheddar cheese

Cook mushroom stems slowly in bouillon for 10 minutes. Discard stems. Saute sliced crowns and onions quickly in 3 tablespoons butter. Combine pork, shrimp, mushrooms, onions, noodles, tomatoes, olives and parsley. Make a white sauce of 1/2 cup butter, 1/3 cup flour, chicken bouillon and 1-1/2 cups milk. Cut cream cheese into small pieces and melt in sauce. Add salt, pepper, thyme and basil. Mix into meat mixture. Spoon into two buttered 2-quart baking dishes. Sprinkle with cheese. Bake in a preheated 350° oven for 30 minutes or until cheese browns slightly and mixture bubbles. Yield: 8-10 large servings.

NOTE: Casseroles can be refrigerated overnight before cooking or they may be frozen.

MENU: Party Pork Casserole, Pickled Carrots, Green Salad, Cottage Cheese, Relishes, Small Buttered Rolls, Assorted Cookies, Coffee.

GARNISH: Sliced ripe olives on greens.

foreign recipes

The following recipes have been adapted to American tastes and markets. Therefore, in the truest sense of the word, we can't call them authentic. Get yourself in the proper mood and you'll find them just foreign enough to change your mealtime routine.

chinese shredded pork and vegetables

1 lb. pork shoulder, shredded
1 tablespoon oil
1 cup chopped green onions, tops too
1 can (16 oz.) bamboo shoots or bean sprouts
1 can (4 oz.) mushrooms, sliced
1 tablespoon sugar
1 tablespoon cornstarch
2 tablespoons soy sauce
2/3 cup mushroom liquid plus chicken bouillon
1 teaspoon ground ginger, or 1 tablespoon fresh sliced ginger
1 can (5 oz.) water chestnuts, sliced lengthwise

Cook pork in oil til no pink shows. Add onions, bamboo shoots and mushrooms. Saute quickly. Combine sugar and cornstarch. Mix in soy sauce and liquid. Add to meat. Heat and stir to thicken slightly. Add ginger and water chestnuts. Heat til hot. Yield: 4 servings.

MENU: Shredded Pork and Vegetables, Snow Peas, Rice, Preserved Fruit on Chopped Ice Mounds, Tea, Milk.

GARNISH: The foods will garnish each other on the plates but are served in separate dishes.

spanish roast pork with seville orange sauce

Pork Roast, any kind or weight
1/2 cup dry white wine
1 tablespoon brown sugar
1/4 cup Cointreau
1/2 cup orange juice
1/2 teaspoon salt
2 teaspoons cornstarch
1 tablespoon water
4 small sweet oranges, sectioned and membranes removed
  (Use 2 small cans of mandarin oranges as a substitute.)

Place roast fat side up on a rack in a shallow pan. Roast in a 325° oven according to the schedule on page 17. Heat liquids and seasonings and boil for 5 minutes. Mix cornstarch and water. Stir into hot liquid. Stir and heat until thickened. Add orange segments. Simmer covered for 10 minutes. Serve hot with roast. Yield: 6-8 servings.

MENU: Roast Pork with Seville Orange Sauce, Green Beans Amandine, Rice, Lettuce and Cucumber Salad, Flan, Coffee, Milk.

GARNISH: Skewer two or three orange sections onto the top of the roast. Use greens on the platter.

german roast pork shoulder with mustard sauce

Roll Pork Shoulder (Picnic)
2 tablespoons prepared mustard, Dijon or Dusseldorf
2 teaspoons white wine vinegar
1/2 teaspoon seasoned salt
1/8 teaspoon white pepper
1/4 cup salad oil
2 tablespoons dill weed
2 teaspoons chopped parsley
2 tablespoons capers

Place roast on rack in a 325° oven. Roast 35 or 40 minutes per pound or until the internal temperature is 170°. Combine mustard, vinegar, salt and pepper. Beat in salad oil. Add dill, parsley and capers. Blend well. Yield: 3/4 cup. Count on 4 servings of roast per pound.

MENU: Roast Pork with Mustard Sauce, Potato Pancakes, Buttered Broccoli, Red and Green Cabbage Slaw, Chocolate Cake, Coffee, Milk.

GARNISH: Broccoli with cherry tomatoes or pimiento strips.

french pork collops with mushrooms

1 lb. fresh mushrooms
1 tablespoon chopped fresh thyme, or 1/2 teaspoon dried
2 cups chicken bouillon
3 tablespoons butter
1 tablespoon olive oil
12 very thin slices (1/4 inch) pork tenderloin
    cut on the diagonal
1 tablespoon cornstarch
2 tablespoons water
1/2 cup light cream
16 toast points (4 slices)
Paprika
Fresh chopped parsley for garnish

Remove mushroom stems. Simmer stems with thyme for 15 minutes in chicken bouillon. Slice the mushroom crowns. Saute them quickly in butter and olive oil. (The olive oil keeps the butter from burning.) Remove the mushrooms from the butter and brown pork quickly on both sides. Return mushrooms to the pork and keep both warm. Strain chicken bouillon. Discard mushroom stems. Mix cornstarch and water. Stir into the bouillon. Heat and stir to boiling. Gradually stir in cream. Heat and stir to simmering. Add pork and mushrooms. Heat thoroughly. Correct seasoning. Serve on toast points. Yield: 4 servings.

LUNCHEON MENU: Pork Collops With Mushrooms, Buttered Asparagus, Sliced Carrots, Tomato and Lettuce a la Goldenrod Salad, Dessert Crepes with Grand Marnier Sauce, Coffee, Milk.

GARNISH: Sprinkle paprika and chopped parsley over sauce.

NOTE: Sauce may be made the day before and stored in the refrigerator. Cook the pork and reheat the sauce at the last minute.

mexican
carnitas with avocado sauce

1 lb. lean pork (1 inch cubes)
1/2 teaspoon monosodium glutamate
Seasoned salt and pepper

Sprinkle pork with monosodium glutamate. Refrigerate for two hours. Place meat on a rack. Roast for 1-1/4 hours in a 250° oven. Sprinkle with seasoning. Cook 45 minutes in a 300° oven. Serve hot with Avocado Sauce. Yield: 4 servings.

Avocado Sauce

1 large tomato, peeled and diced
1 avocado, diced
1 tablespoon finely chopped onion
1 tablespoon red wine vinegar
1-1/2 teaspoons olive oil
1/8 teaspoon monosodium glutamate
Salt and pepper to taste

Combine all ingredients gently. Let stand at room temperature for a half hour. Serve over Carnitas. Yield: 4 servings.

MENU: Carnitas With Avocado Sauce, Mixed Vegetables, Frijoles, Green Salad, Mexican Cookies, Coffee, Milk.

GARNISH: Carnitas with sauce doesn't need to be garnished.

irish
ham with madeira glaze

Ready to Eat Ham (about 10 lbs.)
Whole cloves
1 cup Madeira wine
3/4 cup strained honey

Stud ham with cloves. (Make a hole first with the ice pick, it's easier.) Combine wine and honey. Spread on ham. Heat in 325° oven for about 3 hours or to an internal temperature of 150°. Baste several times. Serve with a Madeira wine sauce (thickened with cornstarch). Yield: 2-3 servings per pound.

MENU: Sliced Baked Ham, Madeira Wine Sauce, Parslied Potatoes, Buttered Green Beans, Sorrel and Watercress Salad, Applesauce Cake, Tea, Milk.

GARNISH: Pickled peaches and watercress.

latvian
pork smothered in onions and sour cream

1/2 pound fresh mushrooms
3 tablespoons butter
1 medium onion, chopped
1 slice (1/2 inch thick) fresh ham steak
Seasoned flour
2/3 cup beef bouillon
1/3 cup sour cream

Slice mushrooms. Saute quickly in butter. Remove mushrooms and brown onions. Remove onions. Trim meat and cut into serving size pieces. Flour and brown meat. Add more butter if necessary. Put mushrooms and onions on meat. Add hot bouillon. Cover and simmer for 30 minutes or until meat is fork tender. Blend 1 teaspoon seasoned flour into sour cream. Stir slowly into bouillon. Heat to just below boiling. Correct seasoning. Yield: 4 servings.

MENU: Pork Smothered in Onions and Sour Cream, Baked Potatoes, Dilled Peas, Pickled Beet and Egg Salad, Apple Dumplings, Tea, Milk.

GARNISH: Cooked julienne carrot sticks sprinkled on top of sauce just before serving.

hungarian
pork chops with sauerkraut

1 small onion, finely chopped
Bacon drippings
1 tablespoon paprika
1 tablespoon caraway seed
4 cups sauerkraut (2 lbs.), rinsed in water
8 thin pork chops
Seasoned flour
1 cup sour cream

Cook onions in drippings til golden. Sprinkle with paprika. Mix caraway seed in sauerkraut. Mix in onion. Cover and simmer while chops are browning. Dust chops with flour seasoned with salt and pepper. Brown on both sides. Place on sauerkraut. Cover. Simmer 1 hour or until meat is tender. Add a few tablespoons of water if necessary. Mix sour cream in sauerkraut about 5 minutes before serving. Yield: 4 servings.

MENU: Pork chops With Sauerkraut, Boiled Potatoes, Dilled Green Beans, Green Salad, Plum Dumplings, Coffee, Milk.

GARNISH: Sour cream

hawaiian stew

2 pounds pork shoulder, cubed
Flour for dusting
Bacon drippings
1 medium onion, chopped
1/2 cup tomato juice
3 large tomatoes, peeled and quartered
1 green pepper, chopped
Salt and pepper
2 medium summer squash, sliced

Dust pork in flour and brown in drippings. Cook onion until wilted. Add tomato juice. Cover. Cook 35 minutes or until pork is tender. Add tomatoes, green pepper, seasoning and squash. Cover and cook 10 minutes or until vegetables are tender. Taste for seasoning. Yield: 4-6 servings.

MENU: Hawaiian Stew, Curried Rice, Sweet Sour Cucumbers, Fresh Chilled Pineapple Wedges, Iced Tea, Milk.

GARNISH: Mint leaves.

danish stuffed spareribs

2 slabs spareribs, trimmed
Seasoned salt and pepper
1 cup mixed dried fruit, chopped
3 tart apples, cored, pared and sliced
1-1/2 cups chicken bouillon

Season meat. Place fruit on 1 slab. Top with other spareribs. Skewer. Brown in hot fat on the surface of the range or in a 375° oven. Add hot bouillon. Bake in a 325° oven for 1-1/2 hours or until tender. Yield: 4 servings.

MENU: Stuffed Spareribs, Gravy, Oven Browned Potatoes, Buttered Cabbage, Danish Pastry, Coffee, Milk.

GARNISH: Serve potatoes around Spareribs. Decorate ribs with dried fruit puffed in a little hot water.

NOTE: The Danish usually use only prunes and apples, but the mixed fruit and apples taste so good. Why not try both?

philippine sliced pork

1 small onion, finely chopped
1 clove garlic, finely chopped
Drippings
3 tablespoons brown sugar
1/2 cup lime juice
1/2 cup water
1/2 teaspoon ginger
1/2 teaspoon seasoned salt
Dash cayenne pepper
1/2 teaspoon cornstarch
1 tablespoon water
1/8 teaspoon shredded lime peel
Roast pork, cooked and sliced, hot or cold

Brown onion and garlic in drippings. Add brown sugar, lime juice and water, ginger, salt and pepper. Cover and simmer 15 minutes to blend flavors. Strain. Mix cornstarch and water. Stir into mixture. Stir and heat to boiling. Add shredded peel. Serve over pork. Yield: about 1 cup.

MENU: Philippine Sliced Pork, Fried Rice, Snow Peas, Banana and Peanut Salad, Pineapple Cream, Tea, Milk.

GARNISH: Lime slices, whole or quartered.

04 dook

6 strips thin sliced bacon
12 pieces pitted dried fruit

Cut bacon in half crosswise. Wrap around each piece of fruit. Be careful not to stretch bacon. Secure with a pick. Broil or cook in a preheated 450° oven for a very few minutes, until the bacon is crisp. Serve hot, but don't burn your tongue! Yield: 12 pieces.

NOTE: The English serve savouries between or after desserts at large dinners, but they are also very nice for appetizers.

barbecuing

Pork is both versatile and tasty for all kinds of outside cookery as well as for rotisserizing in your oven.

selection of cuts

It would probably be easier to name those cuts that wouldn't be suitable. Among the tastiest cuts are steaks, chops, ribs, roasts, ham steaks and roasts and Canadian style Bacon. Have you ever cooked bacon cutlets for breakfast? Irresistible! Pork kabobs are mighty popular, too. The meats should be at least an inch thick. If they aren't, be sure to baste them frequently and not overcook.

the amount of meat to buy

There's something about eating outdoors, with the delicious aromas and fresh air that seems to develop instant giant appetites. Of course you know your family and guests, but usually 3/4 to 1 pound of lean meat or a half a slab of ribs per person isn't a bit too much to plan on.

generalities about barbecuing pork

Pork is cooked when the center is gray white and when there is no pink showing in the center or next to the bone. Sometimes there is a pink ring like the color of ham, around the edge of the meat. This is not the same thing so do not be misled. The ring, incidentally, is harmless.

Because pork should be thoroughly cooked, but not overcooked, it is well to have the meat at room temperature before starting to barbecue. (This is different from roasting meat in the oven.) Refrigerated meat will usually warm to room temperature in an hour. Frozen meats, of course, will take longer to reach the proper temperature.

Start burning the charcoal about 30 minutes before time. They should be completely covered with gray ash and all flames should have died down when they are ready.

For a smokey flavor, soak hickory chips in water while coals are being prepared. Put the wet chips over the coals just before you put the meat on the grill. Fat dripping on the coals cause flame flare-ups, so be sure to cut off all excess fat from the meat.

continued on next page

Be prepared with all of your equipment before starting to barbecue. Once the meat is on the grill, don't leave it for a minute or you'll have flare-ups galore! Have water ready to douse flames. A water pistol is very handy but a laundry sprinkler isn't as much of a temptation for the younger generation to borrow (or maybe to take back).

Follow manufacturer's instructions for the best results with your equipment. It is difficult to give exact cooking times because of such variables as outside temperature, amount of wind and proportion of coals to meat.

Don't skimp on charcoal. Nothing is more frustrating than to be short of hot coals when the meat isn't entirely cooked.

Barbecue for two meals at once. Wrap the second portion in foil with a little extra sauce and store in the refrigerator or freeze. Reheat in the foil for a later meal. This is also a good trick if you're going to entertain a large group or are afraid of bad weather.

Speaking of entertaining, one smart hostess has a repertoire of delicious soups and handsome mugs to bring out in case friend husband's timing is off a half hour or so. How diplomatic!

Hibachis are great to use for just two people. If you want to smoke the meat, poke holes in foil and drape it lightly over the top.

For a better smoke flavor, brush meat with water or salt water until the last 15 or 20 minutes. Then daub with barbecue sauce until the meat is cooked.

pork steaks

Shoulder or fresh ham steaks are delicious as well as economical for barbecuing. Ask your meat dealer to slice them an inch thick. You may have to call him a day or two early, so plan ahead. The steaks should cook in about 40 to 45 minutes, but check the manufacturer's instructions and the other variables mentioned above. The most important check is to make sure that the meat isn't pink in the center or next to the bone.

MENU: Barbecued Pork Steaks, Roast Corn, Potato Salad, Buttered Kohlrabi, Green Apple Pie, Coffee, Milk.

Smoked Ham or Canadian Style Bacon just needs to be brown on the outside and hot on the inside, so the time will be much shorter. Ten to 15 minutes will be about right to think about, but don't forget the variables. Pineapple slices are delightful when you sprinkle a little brown sugar on either side and grill them for just about 5 minutes. Serve them on the ham slices and your reputation will be made. Mix the juice from the canned pineapple slices with 1 teaspoon Dijon mustard, 2 tablespoons honey and 1 teaspoon lemon juice or vinegar for the barbecue sauce.

MENU: Barbecued Ham with Grilled Pineapple, Curried Rice, Mixed Vegetables, Sliced Cucumber and Tomatoes, Chocolate Pudding, Iced Coffee, Milk.

pork chops

Chops can be prepared the same way as pork steaks. They can also be threaded on a *rotisserie* with or without vegetables in between. Brush on your favorite barbecue sauce or a salad dressing periodically.

MENU: Rotisserized Pork Chops and Mushrooms with Italian Dressing, Scalloped Potatoes, Oven-baked Green Beans a la Marjoram, Red and Green Cabbage Slaw, Cantaloupe and ice cream, Coffee, Milk.

bacon cutlets

Have slab bacon sliced 1/2 inch thick. Grill until crisp and brown. This should take 20 minutes or so. Have the eggs ready. This is great for breakfast cookouts in the backyard, in the mountains, or wherever you and your grill happen to be at breakfast time. Plan on plenty.

BREAKFAST COOKOUT MENU: Orange Juice, Crisp Bacon Cutlets, Sunny Eggs, Grilled English Muffins, Raspberry Jam, Coffee, Milk.

pork roasts

Unless the roast has a very small diameter (so to speak), it will be better if it is rotisserized or, if it is very large, cooked by the spit or pit methods. Otherwise, it would be too difficult to cook the meat thoroughly so that all of the pink color would be gone. If rotisserizing the meat, the use of an internal meat thermometer is an easy way to check for doneness. Cook pork to 170° for the best flavor. The length of time will depend on the cut and the equipment. Follow the manufacturer's directions.

continued on next page

MENU: Rotisserie Pork Roast basted with Korean Marinade, Fluffy Rice, Buttered Beets, Crisp Young Spinach Salad, Lemon Cake, Iced Tea, Milk.

Marinades: These are simply sauces that are similiar to barbecue sauces. They usually have some acid to act as a tenderizing agent, some oil to make them cling and flavorings to make them taste good. Meats are usually soaked (marinated), for any length of time from 2 hours to 3 days. After the meat has been removed from the marinade, it can be heated to boiling and served as a sauce. Since marinades rarely spoil, they should never be wasted. Store them in the freezer or refrigerator to be used again.

Commercial Italian Dressing or Vinegar and Oil Dressing are excellent marinades.

Wine Marinade

2-1/2 cups dry red wine
1 large onion, chopped
1 carrot, sliced
1 garlic clove, crushed
1 teaspoon chopped fresh thyme or 1/2 teaspoon dry thyme
1 teaspoon salt
1/2 teaspoon fresh ground pepper
2 tablespoons salad oil

Simmer 15 minutes. Pour over meat. Marinate at least 3 hours or overnight in the refrigerator. After the meat has been roasted, heat the marinade to boiling and use as a sauce. Yield: about 3 cups.

White Wine Marinade

2 cups white wine
2 teaspoons paprika
1 teaspoon salt
2 teaspoons sugar
1/4 teaspoon pepper
1/2 teaspoon onion powder
1/4 teaspoon garlic powder
2 tablespoons salad oil

Simmer 15 minutes. Pour over meat. Let stand in the refrigerator for at least 8 hours. Baste often. After meat has been roasted, heat marinade to boiling and use as a sauce.

Korean Marinade

1 cup soy sauce
1 teaspoon onion juice or 1/2 teaspoon onion powder
1/2 teaspoon garlic juice or 1/4 teaspoon garlic powder
1 bottle (8 oz.) ginger ale
1/2 cup sesame seeds
1/4 cup oil

Combine all ingredients and simmer 10 minutes. Pour over meat. Refrigerate for 3 hours or longer. Baste often. Heat to boiling before using as a sauce. Yield: 2-3/4 cups.

barbecued ribs

Barbecued spareribs are sometimes served as appetizers but are more often served as the entree for delightful outdoor meals. While back ribs and country style backbones aren't used for appetizers, they are prepared and served in the same manner as entrees. All three are probably the most regional foods that are served. In some areas, hot means temperature. The further south and west one goes, however, the more "hot" refers to the seasoning.

Steaming. One friend who makes wonderful ribs, steams them in the oven until they are almost tender. She bastes the ribs with salt water while they are on the grill until the last half hour. During the last 30 minutes, she bastes the ribs with barbecue sauce. This method is supposed to remove the fat, retain juices and prevent the sauce from burning.

Grilling. Others cut most of the excess fat off the ribs and grill them slowly, basting with salt water. Tomato Barbecue Sauce is used the last 30 minutes. This method also keeps the sauce from excessive burning. It also permits more smoke penetration than if the sauce were used from the start.

There are still others who would feel that either of the above methods would be heresy of the very worst order! Turn the ribs at least every 5 minutes, they say, and baste each time with thin barbecue sauce. Do this for an hour and a half or until the meat pulls away from the bone. Serve the rest of the sauce on the side.

Which is correct? Well, how do you like barbecued ribs?

barbecue sauces

Thin Barbecue Sauce

1/2 pound butter
2 cups vinegar
1/2 cup tangy catsup
1/2 cup chili sauce
1/2 cup Worcestershire sauce
1/2 cup water
1 teaspoon dry mustard

1-1/2 teaspoons sugar
1/2 teaspoon salt
1/2 teaspoon red pepper
2 tablespoons chopped onion
4 dashes Tabasco Sauce
1 clove garlic, finely chopped

Mix all ingredients. Simmer 45 minutes to blend seasonings. Yield: 1 quart.

Thick Barbecue Sauce

4 small onions, finely chopped
1/4 cup vinegar
1/4 cup Worcestershire sauce
2 teaspoons seasoned salt

2 teaspoons chili powder
1-1/2 cups tangy catsup
1-1/2 cups water

Cover and simmer all ingredients for 45 minutes. Heat to boiling. Yield: 3-1/2 cups.

Lemon Barbecue Sauce

1 bottle (8 oz.) Italian Style Salad Dressing
1 cup fresh lemon juice
1/2 cup butter
1/2 teaspoon salt
2 teaspoons seasoned salt
2 cloves garlic, mashed
1/4 cup finely chopped onion
1/2 teaspoon dried thyme

Heat to boiling. Let stand in the refrigerator for at least 12 hours before using. Yield: 2-3/4 cups.

NOTE: All of the above sauces can be kept in the refrigerator or the freezer for future use.

Peach Barbecue Sauce

1 cup chili sauce
1 cup (12 oz.) peach or apricot preserves
1/3 cup wine vinegar
1 teaspoon hot dry mustard

Combine all ingredients. Heat to boiling. Let stand 2 hours before using. Yield: 2-1/3 cups.

liver

Pork Liver Piquant

1-1/2 pounds sliced pork liver
Flour for dusting
1 large onion, sliced
4 teaspoons chopped parsley
1/4 cup butter
1/4 cup flour
1/4 teaspoon salt
3 tablespoons vinegar
2-1/2 cups tomato vegetable juice

Dust slices of liver with flour. Brown liver, onion, and 3 teaspoons parsley in butter. Stir in half the flour, salt and vinegar. Add juice gradually. Cover and cook slowly for 20 to 30 minutes or until tender. Remove liver and thicken sauce with the rest of the flour. Sprinkle the rest of the parsley over the liver and sauce. Yield: 6 servings.

pigs feet

Cover feet with cold water. Simmer (don't boil) until fork tender. Count cooking time when water begins to simmer. Meats are more tender it cooked at a simmering rather than at a boiling temperature. The approximate cooking time will be 2 to 3 hours.

Pigs feet are sometimes sold pickled. They are then served cold with picnic-like food.

When pigs feet and hocks are not separated, they are known as Lacones.

pork hocks and knuckles

Hocks and knuckles are cooked and served the same way. Knuckles have more bones than hocks.

Pork Hocks and Sauerkraut

4 pork hocks or knuckles
1 quart sauerkraut
Salt and pepper
Caraway seeds (optional)

Cover hocks with water and bring to a boil. Simmer 1-1/2 hours or until tender. Add sauerkraut and seasonings and cook about 30 minutes. Yield: 4 servings.

NOTE: Cabbage may be substituted for the sauerkraut. If so, cook the hocks with onion and cook the cabbage quickly for only about 10 minutes.

pork cutlets

These are boneless pieces of pork steak and are often frozen. The following recipes require that they be thawed first.

Creole Pork Cutlets

1 pound pork cutlets	*Bacon drippings*
Seasonings	*1 can (16 oz.) tomatoes*
1/8 teaspoon red pepper	*1/2 cup sliced onion*
Flour	*1 cup diced carrots*

Season cutlets. Dip in flour. Roll and fasten with a pick. Brown in drippings. Pour tomatoes over meat. Add onion and carrots. Cover and cook slowly or bake in a 350° oven for 45 minutes or until tender. Yield: 4 servings.

Breaded Pork Cutlets

1 pound pork cutlets	*1 tablespoon water*
1 teaspoon salt	*Sifted crumbs*
1/8 teaspoon pepper	*Shortening*
1 egg, slightly beaten	

Season cutlets. Dip into egg and water mixture, then in crumbs. Brown on both sides. Cover. Cook slowly for about 35 minutes or until cutlets are tender. Add 1 tablespoon of water if necessary. Yield: 4 servings.

smoked pork

Ham

Charles Lamb's immortal account of Bo Bo the unfortunate young Chinese boy who burned both his father's house and pet pig, is probably the first report of smoked and roasted pork. Salting (or curing), smoking and drying were the main methods of meat preservation all over the world until well into the 19th century. Smoked ham has and does form the flavor base of many classic French, Spanish and American dishes. What could be more welcome than a beautifully glazed baked ham or a slice of crispy fried ham with red eye gravy?

Buying

Smoked To-Be-Cooked Ham
Smoked Ready-To-Eat Ham
Country Style Ham
Canned Cured Ham
Canned Smoked and Cured Ham

Selecting

Select the kind and brand that suits you and your family. Hams and most cured meats can be selected most successfully by brand. Each company's cure has its own characteristic flavor that is difficult if not impossible to duplicate exactly. Hams vary in weight from 9 to 22 pounds. Usually, if the hams are properly trimmed, you can count on a heavier ham to yield more meat in proportion to bone.

Economy Hint: If you have a freezer, it's easy for even a small family to use a large ham. Have the hock cut off to cook with navy, green, butter or your favorite kind of beans. Next, have 2 or 3 center slices, about 1/2 or 3/4 inch, sliced for frying or 2 slices 1 inch thick cut for baking. That will leave two nice size roasts for company, for the family or for sandwiches.

Storing

Canned hams vary from 1-1/2 pounds to 17 pounds. Some, usually the smaller ones, don't have to be refrigerated. READ THE LABELS! All hams, except the heavily smoked ones, must be refrigerated at all times except when being cooked or served. (Remember the danger zone of 40° to 140°. Don't let the meat remain in that zone for over 3 hours.) If you plan to keep the ham longer than a week or two, be sure to freeze it.

Freezing

Ham, when properly wrapped in freezer foil or freezer paper, can be frozen successfully for 2 months. After that, if it has been kept frozen, it will be safe to eat but the smoke flavor will weaken. The fat will also have a tendency to turn rancid in several months. Canned hams are not recommended for freezing in the cans.

Thawing

Hams may be thawed in the refrigerator, at room temperature or while cooking.

Roasting

Loosen the skin by running a paring knife under it at the middle of the ham. Slit the skin about 4 inches toward the hock. Do this about every inch around the ham. As it cooks, the skin will curl back toward the hock, but the fat won't be broken. Roast the ham, fat side up, in a 325° oven to 160° internal temperature for the to-be-cooked hams and to 140° for the ready-to-eat hams. The time will vary from 18 to 40 minutes per pound.

Glazing

It's so quick and easy to glaze a ham, picnic or Canadian style Bacon that it's a shame not to do it every time. There are many ways to glaze a ham but this is the tastiest and easiest that we've found. Mix brown sugar (about 2 cups), with about 1 teaspoon dry mustard, 1/4 teaspoon cloves and just enough liquid to make a very thick paste. The liquid may be maraschino cherry juice, fruit juice, the juice from pickled fruit or sherry. Add the liquid a tablespoon at a time because the sugar dissolves at a surprising rate. About an hour or an hour and a half before the ham is finished, spread the mixture on the ham. Stud it with cloves. (Make the holes with an ice pick.) Put the ham in a 325° oven and that's it until it reaches the proper internal temperature.

MENU: Baked Ham, Baked Sweet Potatoes, Buttered Broccoli, Grapefruit and Avocado Salad with French Dressing, Spice Cake a la Mode, Coffee, Milk.

Country hams

These are usually named after the locality where they are cured and smoked. Be sure to follow the label instructions because some are precooked and others need to be soaked and water cooked before baking.

continued on next page

Carve country hams *with* the grain instead of across it. These are highly flavored hams so make the slices paper thin.

MENU: Baked Country Ham, Curried Rice, Wilted Spinach, Molded Cinnamon Applesauce Salad, Lemon Refrigerator Pudding, Coffee, Milk.

NOTE: Consumers sometimes wonder about the amount of juices that flow from the packer style hams as compared with the country style hams. The liquid is what makes the ham mild and tender. Country style hams have heavy curing and smoking to preserve them. Don't forget, country style hams must be soaked, water cooked and then baked in order to make them tender and mild. The amount of liquid in a packer style ham is carefully controlled by consumer preference and by government rules and inspection.

baked ham and ginger pears

1 can (20 oz.) pears
1 teaspoon grated lemon peel
2 tablespoons lemon juice
1/2 teaspoon ginger
1 slice ready-to-eat ham, 2 inches thick
Brown sugar

Remove pears from syrup. Add lemon peel, lemon juice and ginger to pear juice. Boil 5 minutes. Add pears and simmer gently for 5 minutes. Place ham in baking pan 13 x 9 x 2. Pat brown sugar on the surface until it is about 1/4 inch thick. Pour half of the pear syrup around ham. Bake in a 350° oven for 30 minutes or until the meat is heated through. Add the rest of the syrup and arrange pears around the ham slice. Continue baking 15 to 20 minutes until the pears are heated and the syrup has cooked down. Yield: 6 servings. NOTE: For a quicker preparation, use two thinner slices of ham.

MENU: Baked Ham and Ginger Pears, Scalloped Potatoes, Green Beans Amandine, Crisp Garden Salad, Cantaloupe, Iced Tea, Milk.

GARNISH: Pear Halves and Mint leaves.

rosy ham slice

1-1/2 cups applesauce
2 tablespoons red cinnamon candies
1/8 teaspoon ground cloves
1 teaspoon lemon juice
1 slice ready-to-eat ham, 1 inch thick
8 whole cloves

Mix applesauce, candies, ground cloves and lemon juice. Heat until the candies are dissolved. Slash fat around ham in several places. Stud the fat with whole cloves. Place ham in a shallow baking dish. Pour mixture over the ham. Bake in a 350° oven for 45 minutes. Yield: 4 servings.

MENU: Rosy Ham Slice, Baked Potatoes, Zucchini Parmesan, Perfection Salad, Chocolate Cake, Coffee, Milk.

GARNISH: Baked Potatoes and Celery Leaves.

spicy ham slice

1 slice ready to eat ham, 1 inch thick
Whole cloves
1 tablespoon prepared mustard
2 tablespoons brown sugar, firmly packed
1 cup orange juice

Slash fat every inch around the edge of the ham to prevent curling. Stick cloves in fat. Place ham in a shallow baking dish. Mix the mustard and brown sugar together. Spread on the ham slice. Pour orange juice over the ham. Bake in a 350° oven for 40 minutes or until thoroughly heated and browned on top. Yield: 4 servings.

MENU: Spicy Ham Slice, Parsley Potatoes, Buttered Spinach, Waldorf Salad, Baking Powder Biscuits, Honeybutter, Caramel Custard, Coffee, Milk.

GARNISH: Garnish with Parsley Potatoes and tiny bunches of red grapes.

ham slice baked in ginger ale raisin sauce

1 slice ready to eat ham, 1-1/2 inches thick
Cloves
1 tablespoon Dijon mustard
2 tablespoons brown sugar
1 bottle (10 oz.) ginger ale
1 teaspoon cornstarch
1/2 cup seedless raisins

Score fat and stud with cloves. Place ham in baking dish. Spread with mustard. Sprinkle with brown sugar. Pour 1/2 cup ginger ale in baking dish. Bake in a preheated 325° oven for 35 minutes per pound. Combine cornstarch and 1/4 cup ginger ale. Simmer the raisins for 5 minutes in the remaining ginger ale. Add to cornstarch mixture. Cook until thickened and clear. Serve over ham slice. Yield: 6 servings.

MENU: Ham Slice Baked in Ginger Ale Raisin Sauce, Buttered Brown Rice, Peas and Carrots, Sliced Pickled Beets and Sauerkraut Salad, Peach Pie, Coffee, Milk.

GARNISH: Preserved kumquats with parsley.

deviled ham slice

1 slice (1-1/2 lbs.) ready to eat ham, 1/2 inch thick
6 orange slices
1 tablespoon prepared mustard
1/4 teaspoon pepper
1 teaspoon sugar
3 tablespoons vinegar
1/4 cup water

Pan fry ham slice. Place on a warm platter and keep hot. Brown orange slices slightly in drippings. Arrange on platter with ham. Stir into drippings, mustard, pepper, sugar, vinegar and water. Boil 5 minutes and pour over ham. Yield: 6 servings.

MENU: Deviled Ham Slice, Parsley Potatoes, Buttered Broccoli, Tomato Aspic, Lazy Daisy Cake, Tea, Milk.

GARNISH: None needed.

spicy cherry ham slice

1 slice ready to eat ham, 1-1/2 inches thick
Whole cloves
1 can (16 oz.) sour cherries and juice
6 pear halves
1/2 cup brown sugar, firmly packed
1/2 teaspoon cinnamon
1/2 teaspoon allspice
1 tablespoon cornstarch

Score fat. Stick cherries on the fat with cloves. Put ham in a large enough baking dish to allow pears to be placed cut side down around ham. Put remaining cherries on top of ham. Mix sugar and spices. Sprinkle over the top of ham. Make a paste of a small amount of cherry juice and cornstarch. Gradually add the rest of the juice. Pour over the pears. Bake in a preheated 350° oven for 45 minutes. Yield: 6 servings.

MENU: Spicy Cherry Ham Slice, Curry Flavored Rice, Buttered Baby Beets, Crisp Garden Salad, Coffee Ice Cream with Coffee Liqueur, Coffee, Milk.

GARNISH: None necessary.

barbecued ham and beans

1 can (16 oz.) green beans
Fresh ground pepper
1 slice ready to eat ham, 3/4 to 1 inch thick
1/4 cup barbecue sauce

Put beans and 2 tablespoons of liquid from the beans in the bottom of the broiler pan. Season with pepper. Slash fat edges of ham in several places. Put on broiler rack over beans. Brush with half the barbecue sauce. Place the top surface of the meat 4 inches from the source of heat. Broil 5 minutes or until the meat is a golden brown. Turn, brush with the rest of the sauce and broil 5 minutes until golden brown. Yield: 4 servings.

MENU: Barbecued Ham and Beans, Potato Puffs, Molded Pineapple Carrot Salad, German Chocolate Cake, Coffee, Milk.

GARNISH: Cherry Tomatoes

ham and fruit dressing casserole

3 cups croutons
1 egg, beaten
1/2 cup hot water
1/4 cup melted butter or
    margarine
1/4 cup brown sugar,
    firmly packed
1 tart apple

2 teaspoons grated orange peel
2/3 cup orange pulp
    (about 2 oranges)
2/3 cup raisins
1/4 teaspoon cloves
Dash of pepper
6 small slices ready to eat ham,
    1/2 inch thick

Combine croutons with eggs, water, butter and brown sugar. Pare, core and slice apple. Add apple, orange peel, pulp, raisins and seasonings to mixture. Mix well. Put into 2-quart greased baking dish. Top with ham slices. Cover and bake in a preheated 350° oven for about 45 minutes or until the fruit is cooked and ham is thoroughly hot. Yield: 6 servings.

MENU: Ham and Fruit Dressing Casserole, Candied Sweet Potatoes, Buttered Broccoli, Lettuce Wedges with French Dressing, Vanilla Pudding with Chocolate Sauce, Coffee, Milk.

GARNISH: Two thin orange slices cut thru to center and twisted.

glazed ham rolls

6 small cooked sweet potatoes
6 slices ready to eat ham
1/2 cup plus 3/4 cup brown sugar, firmly packed
1 tablespoon butter or margarine
1 tablespoon prepared mustard
1/4 cup orange juice

Place a sweet potato on each slice of ham. Sprinkle each with part of the half cup of brown sugar. Dot with butter. Roll ham around potato and fasten with picks. Place in a buttered shallow baking dish. To make glaze: caramelize 3/4 cup brown sugar. Combine with mustard and orange juice. Cook for 5 minutes. Pour glaze over rolls. Bake in a preheated 350° oven for 30 minutes. Spoon glaze over rolls during the baking period. Yield: 6 servings.

MENU: Glazed Ham Rolls, Asparagus Spears, Buttered Corn, Banana and Peanut Salad, Coconut Custard Pie, Coffee, Milk.

GARNISH: Serve Rolls garnished with Asparagus Spears and Corn.

orange ham rolls

1 cup uncooked chopped cranberries
1/4 cup honey
8 thin slices ready to eat ham
1 cup orange juice
1 tablespoon cornstarch

Combine cranberries and honey. Spread on ham slices to a thickness of 1/4 inch. Roll and secure with picks. Place in a shallow baking dish. Combine orange juice and cornstarch. Pour over ham rolls. Bake for 1 hour in a preheated 350° oven. Yield: 4 servings.

MENU: Orange Ham Rolls, Creamed Potatoes au Gratin, Buttered Mixed Vegetables, Red and White Coleslaw, Pumpkin Pie, Coffee, Milk.

GARNISH: Make a rosette by winding a strip of orange peel about 1 inch wide.

tangy ham slice

1 slice ready to eat ham, 3/4 inch thick
1/8 teaspoon ground cinnamon
1/8 teaspoon ground cloves
1/3 cup brown sugar, firmly packed
1 teaspoon dry mustard
1 teaspoon vinegar
1 large tart apple, shredded

Slash fat edges of ham. Combine seasonings. Add apple. Mix thoroughly. Spread over top of ham. Place in a shallow baking dish. Bake in a preheated 350° oven for 45 minutes. Yield: 4 servings.

MENU: Tangy Ham Slice, Baked Potatoes, Broccoli with Hollandaise Sauce, Garden Salad, Angel Food Cake with Strawberries, Coffee, Milk.

GARNISH: Broccoli

ham and cheese rarebit

1/2 pound shredded cheddar cheese
1 can (10-1/2 oz.) cream of chicken soup
1/4 cup milk
1/4 teaspoon dry mustard
1/2 teaspoon Worcestershire sauce
Dash cayenne pepper
4 pieces toast
4 slices ready to eat ham, 1/4 to 1/2 inch thick

Heat cheese slowly in soup milk mixture until cheese is melted. Add mustard, Worcestershire sauce and cayenne. Continue stirring. When smooth and well blended, pour the rarebit over the toast topped with ham. Yield: 4 servings.

Variations: Chopped olives, ripe or green, may be added to the rarebit. Chopped chives may be used as a topping.

MENU: Ham and Cheese Rarebit, Baked Beans, Wilted Spinach, Carrot and Celery Sticks, Apple Pie, Beverage.

GARNISH: Top each serving with a ripe or a stuffed green olive.

mandarin ham

3/4 cup brown sugar, firmly packed
1/4 teaspoon dry mustard
1 tablespoon cornstarch
1 teaspoon ground ginger
1/4 teaspoon ground cloves
1 clove garlic, minced
1/4 cup vinegar
1/2 cup water
2 cups ready to eat ham cut into 1 inch cubes

Mix together in a skillet all ingredients except ham. Cook about 5 minutes to blend. Add ham. Cook 15 minutes to heat ham. Serve on fluffy rice. Yield: 4 servings.

MENU: Mandarin Ham, Fluffy Rice, Buttered Asparagus Spears, Tossed Salad, French Bread, Blueberry Pie a la Mode, Beverage.

GARNISH: Celery leaves and radish roses.

ham and egg delight

1-1/2 cups cubed ready to eat ham
1/2 cup chopped sauteed mushrooms
2 hard cooked eggs, chopped
3 tablespoons butter or margarine
3 tablespoons flour
1-1/2 cups milk
1/2 teaspoon salt
1/4 teaspoon dill weed

Combine ham and mushrooms. Add eggs to ham mixture. Heat butter and blend in flour. Add milk slowly and stir and heat until blended and boiling. Add ham and seasonings. Heat thoroughly. Serve in toast baskets, or in pattie shells. Yield: 6 servings.

TOAST BASKETS: Cut crusts from 6 slices white bread. Fit bread into buttered muffin tins and brown in the oven.

MENU: Ham and Egg Delight, Green Beans Amandine, Sliced Tomato Salad, Brownies a la Mode, Beverage.

GARNISH: Serve this menu for a luncheon and serve on individual plates with pickled fruit or chutney for an accent.

ham and mushroom casserole

1-1/2 cups uncooked noodles
2 cups medium white sauce
1/2 cup shredded cheddar cheese
1 tablespoon diced onion
1/2 cup chopped celery
1/2 cup (4 oz.) sliced mushrooms
1-1/2 cups diced ready to eat ham
1/2 cup buttered crumbs

Cook noodles in boiling water until tender. Melt cheese in white sauce. Add onion, celery, mushrooms, noodles and ham. Place in a buttered baking dish and cover with crumbs. Bake in a 375° oven for 30 minutes or until the dish is bubbly and browned on top. Yield: 4 servings.

MENU: Ham and Mushroom Casserole, Buttered Mixed Vegetables, Molded Sour Cherry and Pecan Salad, Gingerbread with Whipped Cream, Beverage.

GARNISH: Put a couple of cherry tomatoes on a sprig of parsley over to one side of the casserole.

ham-yam casserole

1 can (10-1/2 oz.) cream of mushroom soup
1/8 teaspoon pepper
1 teaspoon Dijon mustard
3 cups cubed ready to eat ham
3 medium yams, cooked
5 marshmallows

Mix soup, pepper and mustard. Heat and stir until smooth. Add ham and mix thoroughly. Place in a buttered 2-quart casserole. Beat yams until light and fluffy. Pile lightly on top of creamed meat. Cut four of the marshmallows in half and place in a circle on top of yams. Put the fifth one in the center. Bake in a 350° oven for about 30 minutes or until brown on top. Yield: 6 servings.

MENU: Ham-Yam Casserole, Buttered Cauliflower, 3 Bean Salad, Chocolate Ice Cream, Beverage.

GARNISH: Green Pepper Rings.

colorful creamed ham

2 cups cubed ready to eat ham
1/4 cup butter or margarine
1/4 cup chopped celery leaves
1/4 cup flour
2 cups milk.

Brown ham slightly in butter. Add celery leaves and stir to wilt slightly. Blend in flour. Add milk slowly. Stir over low heat until sauce has thickened and reached the boiling point. Taste for seasoning. Serve on hot buttered toast. Yield: 4 servings.

MENU: Colorful Creamed Ham on Toast, Parsley Potatoes, Buttered Peas, Sliced Tomatoes and Cottage Cheese Salad, Peach Cobbler, Beverage.

GARNISH: Celery Leaves.

deluxe ham and corn bake

1/4 cup butter or margarine
2 cups cubed ready to eat ham
1/4 cup finely chopped green pepper
1/2 cup finely chopped celery
1/2 cup finely chopped onion
2 tablespoons brown sugar
2 tablespoons flour
3/4 cup chili sauce
1/2 cup water
1 tablespoon vinegar
1 can (16 oz.) cream style corn
1/2 cup crushed potato chips

Melt butter in a heavy skillet. Brown ham, green pepper, celery and onion. Stir in sugar and flour. Add chili sauce, water and vinegar. Cook slowly until mixture thickens. Mix in corn. Pour into a buttered 2-quart casserole. Top with potato chips. Bake in a 350° oven for 40 minutes or until mixture is brown and bubbling. Yield: 4 servings.

MENU: Deluxe Ham and Corn Bake, Garden Fresh Spinach, Raisin and Carrot Salad, Burned Sugar Cake, Beverage.

GARNISH: Green Pepper Rings.

ham and green bean skillet

1/2 cup chopped onion
2 tablespoons butter or margarine
1 tablespoon flour
3/4 cup liquid from green beans
1 cup shredded cooked ham
1 can (16 oz.) green beans
1/8 teaspoon pepper
1/2 teaspoon dried savory

Cook onions in butter in a heavy skillet. Add flour. Blend. Stir in liquid and stir and cook 'til it boils and thickens. Add other ingredients. Cook slowly for 15 minutes to blend flavors. Yield: 4 servings.

MENU: Ham and Green Bean Skillet, Rice Pilaf, Buttered Beets, Perfection Salad, Butterscotch Cream Pie, Beverage.

GARNISH: Cranberry relish.

easy ham and potatoes in foil

4 medium baking potatoes
2 cups cubed cooked ham
3 tablespoons butter or margarine
Salt and Pepper
1/2 cup chopped parsley
1/2 cup shredded cheddar cheese
1/2 cup light cream

Pare potatoes and cut lengthwise in strips as for french fries. Place potatoes and ham in the center of a large piece of heavy aluminum foil. Shape foil to form baking dish. Dot potatoes with butter. Sprinkle with salt, pepper, 1/4 cup parsley and cheese. Pour cream over. Bring edges of foil up to cover potatoes. Seal all edges to make a tightly closed package but don't press. Place on cookie sheet or shallow pan. Bake in a 425° oven 40 to 50 minutes until potatoes are tender. Sprinkle with extra parsley just before serving. Yield: 4 servings. NOTE: Frozen french fries can be used in this recipe.

MENU: Easy Ham and Potato Au Gratin, Garden Peas and Mushrooms, Sunshine Salad, Date Pudding, Beverage.

GARNISH: A spiced crab apple on each plate.

escalloped ham and pineapple

2 cups cooked cubed ham
3 tablespoons finely chopped onion
3 tablespoons drippings
2 cups crushed pineapple
1-1/2 tablespoons cornstarch
1 teaspoon mint sauce
4 slices hot buttered toast

Brown ham and onions in hot drippings in skillet. Combine pineapple and cornstarch. Heat until thickened and clear. Add mint sauce. Add pineapple mixture to ham. Bring to boil. Cover and simmer for 15 minutes. Stir occasionally. Serve hot over toast sticks or squares. Yield: 4 servings.

MENU: Escalloped Ham and Pineapple, Baked Potatoes, Sauteed Zucchini, Pink Grapefruit and Avocado Salad, Apple Crisp, Beverage.

GARNISH: None necessary.

green peppers stuffed with ham and corn

2 cups cubed cooked ham
1 can (16 oz.) whole kernel yellow corn
1/4 teaspoon celery salt
1 can (10-1/2 oz.) cream of mushroom soup
4 medium green peppers.

Combine ham, corn, celery salt and mushroom soup. Cut the stem and ends from green peppers. Remove the seeds and membrane. Parboil in rapidly boiling salted water. Remove before completely tender (about 5 minutes). Fill with ham and corn mixture. Place about 1/4 cup water in a baking dish. Place green peppers in baking dish. Bake in a 350° oven for 30 minutes. Yield: 4 servings.

MENU: Green Peppers Stuffed With Ham and Corn, Potato Puffs, Sauteed Cherry Tomatoes, Green Salad, Caramel Custard, Beverage.

GARNISH: None needed.

ham and curried rice

1/4 cup butter or margarine
1/2 cup chopped onion
1/2 cup chopped celery
1 chicken bouillon cube
1-1/2 cups hot water
3 cups cooked cubed ham
1/2 cup uncooked rice
1/2 teaspoon curry powder
1/4 teaspoon pepper
1/4 teaspoon paprika
1/2 cup chopped parsley

Brown onion and celery in butter. Dissolve bouillon cube in water. Add ham and all remaining ingredients except parsley. Cover and simmer 30 minutes or until rice is tender. Add parsley and mix. Serve hot. Yield: 4 servings.

MENU: Ham and Curried Rice, Glazed Whole Carrots, Molded Fruit Salad, Marble Cake, Beverage.

GARNISH: The carrots will garnish the ham and rice.

ham and egg supreme

2 tablespoons finely chopped onion
2 tablespoons chopped green pepper
3 tablespoons butter or drippings
3 tablespoons flour
2 cups milk
1/2 teaspoon dry mustard
2 cups cubed cooked ham
2 hard cooked eggs, sliced
1 can (4 oz.) mushrooms, drained

Pan fry onion and green pepper in butter in a heavy skillet. Stir in flour. Save enough milk to make a paste with salt and mustard. Add milk slowly. Bring to a boil over low heat stirring constantly. Stir in milk paste. Add remaining ingredients. Heat thoroughly, about 10 minutes. Serve on hot buttered toast. Yield: 4 to 6 servings.

MENU: Ham and Egg Supreme, Buttered Toast, Tossed Green Salad, Berries and Cream, Beverage.

GARNISH: Small Pickled Peppers.

our best sour cream ham skillet

5 cups cooked ham strips
2 tablespoons drippings
3 tablespoons flour
2 teaspoons dry mustard
1 chicken bouillon cube
2 cups hot water
1 cup sour cream
1 pkg. (8 oz.) noodles, cooked

Brown ham in drippings. Add flour and mustard. Blend. Dissolve bouillon cube in hot water. Add to ham. Stir and cook 'til thickened. Cook 15 minutes to thoroughly blend flavors. Add sour cream. Stir and heat. Do not boil. Taste for seasonings. Serve over hot noodles. Yield: 6 servings.

MENU: Our Best Sour Cream Ham Skillet, Mashed Potatoes, Green Peas, Mandarin Orange Molded Salad, German Chocolate Cake, Beverage.

GARNISH: Parsley.

california style ham loaf

2 cups finely chopped cooked ham
1 cup sliced ripe olives
1 egg, slightly beaten
1/2 cup shredded carrots
1/4 cup finely chopped onion
1/4 cup finely chopped celery
1/4 cup milk
1/4 teaspoon pepper
1/2 cup bread crumbs

Mix all ingredients together. Lightly pack into a buttered 1-quart loaf pan. Bake in a preheated 350° oven for 40 minutes or until browned. Yield: 4 servings.

MENU: California Style Ham Loaf, Parsley Buttered Potatoes, Creamed Spinach, Sweet Sour Tomato Salad, Fresh Plum Pie, Beverage.

GARNISH: Celery leaves and ripe olives.

cheesy ham loaf

2 cups finely chopped cooked ham
2 cups shredded cheddar cheese
2 tablespoons finely chopped green pepper
1/4 cup finely chopped onion
4 eggs, beaten

Mix all ingredients thoroughly. Pack into a buttered, 1-quart loaf pan. Bake in a preheated 350° oven, for 50 minutes or until brown and thoroughly hot. Yield: 4 servings.

MENU: Cheesy Ham Loaf, Buttered Summer Squash, Sweet Sour Green Beans, Cottage Cheese on Peach Halves, Green Apple Pie, Beverage.

GARNISH: Sliced Stuffed Olives on top of the loaf. Greens on the sides.

individual ham loaves with gingersnap sauce

2-1/4 cups ground cooked ham
1/3 cup cracker crumbs
1 egg
1/4 cup diced onion
1/4 cup milk
Dash of pepper
1/4 teaspoon dried thyme

Combine all ingredients. Mix thoroughly. Shape into 4 loaves and place in a buttered shallow pan. Bake in a preheated 350° oven for 20 minutes. Top with Gingersnap Sauce.

Gingersnap Sauce

2 gingersnaps
1/2 lemon
2 tablespoons seedless raisins
1/4 cup brown sugar, firmly packed
3/4 cup hot water
2 tablespoons vinegar

Crush gingersnaps. Cut lemon in thin slices. Mix all ingredients together. Heat to boiling and simmer 15 minutes or until lemon slices are transparent. Stir frequently. Serve over ham loaves. Yield: 4 servings.

MENU: Individual Ham Loaves with Gingersnap Sauce, Buttered Kohlrabi, Baby Carrots, Red Cabbage Slaw, Cheese Cake, Beverage.

GARNISH: Mint leaves and radishes.

ham loaf with parsley sauce

3 cups ground cooked ham
1/2 cup rolled oats
3/4 cup tomato soup
1 egg
1/2 teaspoon allspice
1/4 cup finely chopped parsley
1/4 cup finely chopped green pepper
1 tablespoon finely minced onion

Mix all ingredients together. Pack into a lightly greased 1-quart loaf pan. Bake in a preheated 325° oven for 1 hour. Let stand 5 minutes before removing from pan.

Parsley Sauce

1/4 cup ham drippings
1/4 cup flour
1/4 teaspoon salt
2 cups milk
1/2 cup chopped parsley

Heat drippings in skillet. Blend in flour. Add salt. Add milk gradually. Cook and stir over very low heat until sauce boils. Taste for seasoning. Serve over ham loaf. Sprinkle with chopped parsley. Yield: 4 servings, 1-3/4 cups sauce.

MENU: Ham Loaf With Parsley Sauce, Buttered Potatoes, Peas and Mushrooms, Apricots with Cream Cheese-nut filling, Sunshine Cake, Beverage.

GARNISH: Buttered Potatoes with Parsley Sauce.

snappy ham and cheese patties

2 cups finely chopped cooked ham
12 cheese crackers, crushed (1/2 cup)
1 egg
1/4 teaspoon pepper
1/4 cup catsup
1 tablespoon milk
2 tablespoons shortening

Combine all ingredients except shortening. Shape into 6 patties. Heat shortening. Pan-fry patties 10 minutes on each side or until browned. Yield: 6 patties.

MENU: Snappy Ham and Cheese Patties, Hot Potato Salad, Buttered Spinach, Waldorf Salad, Custard Pie, Beverage.

GARNISH: Serve Patties with the Buttered Spinach.

ham and potato patties

2 cups ground cooked ham
1 egg, beaten
2 cups grated raw potato
1 teaspoon dry mustard
1 tablespoon horseradish
3 tablespoons drippings

Mix ham, egg, potato, and seasonings. Melt drippings in a heavy skillet. Drop mixture from a spoon into skillet, forming 6 (3 inch) patties. Brown slowly on both sides. Add remaining drippings as needed. Serve hot with applesauce. Yield: 6 patties.

MENU: Ham and Potato Patties, Succotash, Buttered Green Cabbage, Molded Cranberry Relish Salad, Peppermint Candy Ice Cream, Beverage.

GARNISH: Serve Patties and Succotash on the same platter with something red — pimiento, pickled peppers or spiced apples.

ham cheese croquettes

2 cups finely chopped cooked ham
1 cup plus 1/2 cup corn flakes
1/4 teaspoon celery seed
1 tablespoon Worcestershire sauce
2 tablespoons onion juice
1/8 teaspoon pepper
1/2 teaspoon curry powder
1/2 cup shredded cheddar cheese
1 egg
3 tablespoons drippings or shortening

Thoroughly mix ham, 1 cup corn flakes, celery seed, Worcestershire sauce, onion juice, pepper, curry powder, cheese and egg. Shape into 8 patties, towers, cylindrical bars or whatever shape you like patties to be. Dip patties into remaining corn flakes. Heat drippings in a heavy skillet. Brown patties on both sides. Serve with parsley sauce.

Parsley Sauce: Add 1 tablespoon chopped parsley to 1 cup medium white sauce made from 2 tablespoons butter, 2 tablespoons flour and 1 cup milk. Yield: 8 croquettes and 1 cup sauce.

MENU: Ham Cheese Croquettes, Buttered Mashed Hominy, Orange Beets, Garden Green Salad, Chocolate Cream Pie, Beverage.

GARNISH: Celery Greens.

ham cheese fondue

1-1/2 cups milk
2 tablespoons butter or margarine
1 cup soft bread crumbs
1 chopped pimiento
2 tablespoons minced parsley
1-1/2 cups shredded cheese
1/8 teaspoon paprika
3 eggs, well beaten
2 cups cooked cubed ham

Heat milk with margarine. Pour over bread crumbs in mixing bowl. Add pimiento, parsley, cheese, pepper and paprika. Mix well. Slowly stir in eggs. Arrange ham in buttered 1-1/2-quart casserole. Pour egg mixture over ham. Set casserole in a large pan and put in the oven. Pour warm water in pan to within 1 inch of the top of casserole. Bake in a preheated 325° oven for 1-1/2 hours or until a table knife inserted 1 inch from the edge is clean when removed from the fondue. Yield: 4 servings.

MENU: Ham Cheese Fondue, Dilled Peas, Lyonnaise Potatoes, Sliced Tomatoes and Cucumbers, Peach Shortcake, Beverage.

GARNISH: Sprinkle paprika on top of Fondue just before serving if it doesn't seem to be brown enough.

french fried ham rolls

8 slices buttered bread
1 tablespoon Dijon mustard
1 cup finely chopped cooked ham
2 eggs, beaten
2 tablespoons butter or margarine

Spread bread with mustard. Spread with ham. Fold and fasten with picks. Dip in egg. Heat butter and brown rolls. Serve hot with mushroom sauce or cheese sauce. Yield: 4 servings.

MENU: French Fried Ham Rolls, Parsley Potatoes, Buttered Carrots, Tossed Green Salad, Lemon Custard, Beverage.

GARNISH: Stick a pick through a stuffed green olive into each roll.

stuffed ham pie

2 cups finely chopped cooked ham
1/2 cup milk
2 cups soft bread cubes
1/2 cup shredded carrots
1/4 cup finely chopped celery
1 tablespoon finely chopped onion
1/2 teaspoon poultry seasoning
1 can (10-1/2 oz.) cream of mushroom soup

Mix ham and milk. Make a stuffing of all remaining ingredients except soup. Place half of meat mixture in an 8-inch pie plate. Place stuffing on top of meat. Top with remaining meat. Pack firmly. Bake in a preheated 400° oven for 25 minutes. Heat soup and spoon over wedge-shaped servings. Yield: 4 servings.

MENU: Stuffed Ham Pie, Baked Sweet Potatoes, Pennsylvania Dutch Spinach, Tomato Aspic, Apple Dumplings, Beverage.

GARNISH: If serving at the table, place a sprig of parsley and a cherry tomato in the center of the pie. It will be easier if you make the cuts in the kitchen.

three layer ham loaf

2 cups finely chopped cooked ham
2 tablespoons finely chopped onion
1 egg
1/8 teaspoon pepper
1 teaspoon Worcestershire sauce
Pinch comino (optional, see herbs)
1 tablespoon finely chopped green pepper
1 tablespoon and 1 tablespoon catsup
1 cup mashed potatoes.

Combine ham, onion, egg, pepper, Worcestershire sauce, comino and green pepper. Mix thoroughly. Place half of mixture in a buttered 10 x 5 x 3 inch loaf pan. Spread with 1 tablespoon catsup. Spread potatoes on top. Cover with remaining meat mixture. Top with 1 tablespoon catsup. Bake in a preheated 350° oven for 35 minutes. Serve hot. Yield: 4 servings.

MENU: Three Layer Ham Loaf, Corn O'Brien, Julienne Cooked Beet and Carrot Salad, Vinaigrette Dressing, Strawberry Bavarian Cream, Beverage.

GARNISH: Serve loaf with the baked tomatoes that are topped with herb flavored crumbs.

sunday
night
ham pie

Pastry

1-1/4 cups sifted flour
1/4 cup cornmeal
1/8 teaspoon sugar
2/3 cup butter
4 tablespoons milk

Sift dry ingredients into mixing bowl. Cut in butter. Add milk 1 tablespoon at a time. Toss with a fork until flour mixture begins to form lumps about 1 inch in diameter. Turn onto a square of wax paper. Shape into a ball. Chill. Roll 1/8 inch thick and put in a 9-inch pie pan. Bake in a preheated 425° oven for 10 minutes.

Filling

2 cups finely chopped cooked ham
1-1/2 cups chopped onion
2 eggs, beaten
1 egg yolk, beaten
3/4 cup sour cream
1/2 teaspoon salt
1/8 teaspoon pepper
1 teaspoon chopped chives or green onion tops
1/4 teaspoon caraway seed.

Brown ham in skillet. Add onions. Cook until soft but not brown. Drain. Combine all ingredients. Pour into partially baked crust. Bake in a preheated 350° oven for 30 minutes or until firm. Test by inserting a table knife half way between edge and center. Serve hot. Yield: 6 servings.

MENU: Sunday Night Ham Pie, Curried Rice, Snow Peas, Pickled Peach, Almond Brittle Cake, Beverage.

GARNISH: Top pie with chopped chives or onion tops and perhaps a dollop of sour cream in the middle.

spiced ham balls

Ham balls

1-1/2 cups ground cooked ham
1/4 cup fine bread crumbs
1 egg
1/2 cup milk
1 teaspoon Worcestershire sauce
1 tablespoon prepared mustard

Combine ham, bread crumbs, egg, milk and seasonings. Mix until thoroughly blended. Shape into 6 balls and put in a buttered shallow baking dish. Bake in a preheated 350° oven for 30 minutes. Yield: 6 balls.

Sweet-sour sauce

2 tablespoons flour
1/3 cup brown sugar
1/3 cup dark corn syrup
2/3 cup water
2 tablespoons vinegar
6 whole cloves

Combine all ingredients for sauce. Heat and stir until slightly thickened. Pour sauce over balls and continue baking for 15 minutes until balls have browned. Yield: About 1-1/2 cups.

MENU: Spiced Ham Balls, Herbed Carrots, Southern-style Green Beans, Stuffed Prune Salad, Chocolate Pudding, Beverage.

GARNISH: Serve the Ham Balls, Carrots and Green Beans on one platter.

ham scrapple

1 cup cornmeal
1 tablespoon sugar
1/2 teaspoon salt
2-1/2 cups boiling water
1/2 cup hot milk
2 cups finely chopped cooked ham
1-1/2 teaspoons prepared mustard
1 tablespoon drippings

Mix together cornmeal, sugar and salt. Add cornmeal mixture slowly to boiling water. Add milk. Stir occasionally. Cook 20 minutes to cook cornmeal. Add ham and mustard. Mix well. Pack into a 9-1/2 x 5-1/4 x 2-3/4 loaf pan. Chill. When cold and firm slice into 1-inch slices. Fry slices in drippings until brown on both sides. Yield: 8 slices.

MENU: Sliced Bananas in Fresh Orange Juice, Ham Scrapple, Creamy Scrambled Eggs, Buttered English Muffins, Ginger Marmalade, Coffee, Milk.

GARNISH: Serve the scrapple on a platter with scrambled eggs.

ham cheese snacks

1-1/2 pounds finely chopped ham
2 tablespoons finely chopped onion
2 tablespoons catsup
1/2 teaspoon garlic salt
4 English Muffins
8 slices of peeled tomato (1/4 inch thick)
4 slices processed cheese
Pinch each of basil and oregano

Combine ham, onion, catsup and garlic salt. Split muffins and toast. Place on baking sheet and top each with a tomato slice. Spread ham mixture over tomato slices. Cut cheese into wide strips. Crisscross ham with cheese. Sprinkle with basil and oregano. Bake in a preheated 400° oven for 15 minutes. Yield: 4 servings.

MENU: Ham Cheese Snacks, Shoestring Potatoes, Pickled Beets, Deviled Eggs, Relish Tray, Fresh Pineapple and Strawberries, Beverage

GARNISH: Parsley or Celery Tops with Radishes and Gherkins.

ham 'n cheese buns

1-1/4 cups finely chopped cooked ham
3/4 cup shredded cheddar cheese
1 tablespoon vinegar
2 tablespoons salad dressing
1/2 teaspoon onion juice
6 frankfurt buns, split and buttered

Combine all ingredients except buns. Fill buns with mixture. Put buns on a cooky sheet and heat in a preheated 375° oven for 10 minutes or until cheese begins to melt. Yield: 6 buns.

MENU: Ham 'N Cheese Buns, Baked Beans, Carrot Sticks, Dill Pickles, Fresh Fruit, Beverage.

crunchy ham salad

1/4 cup mayonnaise
1 tablespoon pickle juice
2 tablespoons diced sweet pickle
2 cups cubed cooked ham
1/2 cup diced celery
1/2 cup cooked peas, chilled
1 cup coarsely crushed potato chips

Mix mayonnaise with pickle juice. Combine with ham, pickle, celery and peas. Just before serving add potato chips and mix. Serve on crisp greens. Yield: 4 servings.

MENU: Crunchy Ham Salad, Corn on the Cob, Sliced Tomatoes and Cucumbers, Blackberry Roly Poly, Beverage.

GARNISH: Poke whole gherkins into the top of the salad.

ham mousse

2 eggs
1 envelope unflavored gelatin
1/4 cup cold water
1/2 cup boiling water
2 tablespoons lemon juice
2 cups chopped cooked ham
1/4 cup chopped sweet pickle
1 tablespoon minced onion
2 tablespoons mayonnaise
1/2 cup heavy cream

Hard cook eggs. Soften gelatin in cold water. Dissolve in hot water. Add lemon juice. Chill until partially set. Chop eggs fine. Combine with ham, pickle, onion and mayonnaise. Stir into gelatin mixture. Whip cream and fold into mixture. Pour into individual molds or 2-quart ring mold. Chill until firm. Unmold and serve on lettuce.

MENU: Ham Mousse filled with Green Salad, Cooked Salad Dressing, Potato Salad, Vinaigrette Asparagus, Peach Ice Cream, Raspberry Sauce, Beverage.

GARNISH: Put peeled, quartered tomatoes around the mousse.

fried ham

1 slice ready to eat ham, 1/2 inch thick
Drippings

Cut Ham into 4 portions. Brown quickly in hot drippings. Remove ham to a warm platter.

pan gravy

Quickly add 1/2 to 3/4 cup warm water to skillet and stir to loosen all the brown bits. Spoon over ham.

red eye gravy

There are many versions of this gravy but the most colorful recommends 1 cup strong coffee and 1 oz. bourbon along with thickening be added to the drippings. You're on your own with this recipe! Generally, Red Eye refers to pan gravy.

milk gravy

Use ham or bacon drippings and half milk and half water. Make it just like a medium white sauce. If the gravy gets too thick, add a little more liquid. Taste for seasoning and don't forget to use a little white pepper. This is mighty tasty, nutritious and quick.

MENU. Fried Ham, Milk Gravy, Boiled Potatoes, Buttered Peas and Onions, Baking Powder Biscuits, Warm Cherry Pie, Beverage.

GARNISH: This can be garnished with greens or with spiced crab apples.

boneless smoked pork shoulder

These are known by various names but if you read the labels you'll find which cuts of meats are the pork shoulder butts or rolls. They vary in weight from about 12 oz. to 3 or 4 pounds and are rectangular in shape.

They can be prepared in a variety of ways and are appropriate to serve on many occasions. The shoulder butts are boneless, but they do have a little fat between the portions of lean so count on approximately 4 to 4-1/2 oz. per serving.

Pork Shoulder Butts taste best when they are water cooked before being finished by other methods.

To Water Cook: Place shoulder butt in water to cover. Simmer about 45 minutes to the pound. For a "boiled" dinner, vegetables may be added during the last half hour of cooking.

To Oven Cook: Place meat on rack in roasting pan. Bake in a 325° oven about 55 minutes per pound.

Glazed Roast: Cook by one of the above methods. Cover with a glaze such as orange marmalade or brown sugar and honey. Bake in a 400° oven for 15 minutes.

To Pan-Fry: Place thin slices of meat in cold frying pan. Cook over low heat until well browned on both sides.

smoked shoulder and cauliflower fare

2 cups cooked cubed smoked shoulder
1 cup cooked cauliflower pieces
1 can (10-1/2 oz.) cream of celery soup
1/2 cup milk
1/4 cup and 1/4 cup shredded cheese
1/2 teaspoon dried savory

Combine meat, cauliflower, soup diluted with milk, 1/4 cup cheese and savory. Pour into buttered 1-1/2-quart casserole. Top with remaining cheese. Bake in a preheated 350° oven for 40 minutes or until the cheese is melted and browned. Yield: 4 servings.

MENU: Smoked Shoulder and Cauliflower Fare, Oven Fried Potatoes, Tomato Aspic, Pineapple Upside Down Cake, Beverage.

GARNISH: If cheese isn't brown, sprinkle with paprika.

shoulder roll slices with apple kraut

6 slices (1/2 inch) cooked shoulder roll
1 can (29 oz.) sauerkraut
1 teaspoon caraway seed
1/2 cup brown sugar
1-1/2 cups sliced unpared apples

Brown meat slices in a skillet. Combine sauerkraut, caraway seeds and brown sugar. Remove meat slices from skillet. Place sauerkraut mixture in bottom of skillet. Cover with apple slices. Place meat on top. Cover and simmer 25 minutes or until apples are soft. Yield: 6 servings.

MENU: Sliced Smoked Shoulder Roll with Apple Kraut, Glazed Carrots, Baked Potatoes, Pear and Cheddar Cheese Salad, Hot Spice Cake, Lemon Sauce, Beverage.

GARNISH: None needed.

fruited shoulder roll slices

6 slices cooked Shoulder Roll, 1/2 inch thick
3 pineapple rings
6 canned apricots
6 tablespoons honey

Place slices on a broiler rack. Place 1/2 pineapple slice and 1 apricot on each slice of meat. Coat each with one tablespoon honey. Broil 3 inches from the source of heat for 12 minutes or until well browned. Yield: 6 servings.

MENU: Fruited Shoulder Roll Slices, Parsley Buttered Potatoes, Cauliflower with Cheese Sauce, Crisp Green Salad, Black Walnut Cake, Beverage.

GARNISH: None needed.

smoked picnics

Picnics are smoked shoulder cuts of Pork and may be purchased in both the to-be-cooked style and the ready-to-eat style. Weights vary from 5 pounds to 8 pounds. Cook them just like ham, to an internal temperature of 170° for the uncooked kind and to 140° for the cooked variety. Plan on 35 minutes to the pound for the uncooked picnics and 25 to 30 minutes to the pound for those that are fully cooked.

About an hour before the picnic is cooked, remove it from the oven, remove the skin and cover the fat with one of the following mixtures:

 2/3 cup brown sugar and 1 tablespoon flour
 2/3 cup brown sugar and 1 tablespoon prepared mustard.
Bake it in the same 325° oven for one hour.

picnic and sweet potato casserole

2 cups cooked sweet potatoes
2 tablespoons drippings
1/4 teaspoon salt
1/8 teaspoon nutmeg
1/3 cup orange juice
2 cups diced cooked picnic

Mash sweet potatoes. Mix with drippings, salt, nutmeg and orange juice. Mix in picnic. Put in buttered casserole. Dot the top with butter. Bake in a preheated 350° oven for 45 minutes or until thoroughly heated and browned on top. Yield: 4 servings.

MENU: Picnic and Sweet Potato Casserole, Buttered Mixed Vegetables, Perfection Salad, Brownies a la Mode, Beverage.

GARNISH: Ring the outside of the casserole with small marshmallows.

canadian style bacon

This is the cured and smoked eye of the rib and the loin. It may be purchased sliced or in a large piece. It has no bone and very little fat, so waste is practically nil.

sliced

The trick here is to put the meat in a very hot skillet and to fry it quickly. Serve sliced Canadian Style Bacon with breakfast (or lunch or supper) eggs. There is little discernable fat to disturb your conscience or diet and it is a nice change with eggs.

Eggs Benedict that elegant breakfast dish depends on Canadian Style Bacon for the meat. The rest of the recipe, by the way, is: a half toasted English muffin topped with the meat, topped with a poached egg, topped with Hollandaise Sauce. It's mighty impressive and tasty.

in one piece

This method of cooking serves many purposes—all of them good.

For two or three persons, purchase a piece 6 or 8 inches long. Glaze it just like ham. Heat in a 400° oven for 30 to 45 minutes. Plan on 3 to 4 slices per ample serving.

Time two or more pieces of Canadian Style Bacon to be ready 15 or 20 minutes apart for a reception. Serve the meat with party style rye bread and let your guests carve for themselves. The meat will stay hot and the men will bless you for serving substantial food.

bacon

Bacon varies in the thickness, the amount of smoke and the amount of fat. Thin sliced bacon is usually the leanest. It is sometimes referred to as, "hotel style". Thick sliced bacon is usually the fattest and has the heaviest smoke. It is called, "Country Style", "Old Fashioned" or, amazing enough, "Thick Sliced."

Slab bacon is unsliced bacon which you can buy and slice yourself or ask the meat man to slice it the thickness that you and your family like best.

Selecting

What is thick and what is thin in bacon?

Thin or Hotel slice	18 to 32 slices per pound
Regular slice	16 to 18 slices per pound
Thick slice	14 to 16 slices per pound

Not all stores carry all three kinds of bacon.

Buying

If you buy by national brand you will be able to select your favorite wherever you go. However, your meat dealer will be able to help you select your favorite style from among the many fine local brands. Naturally they will be government inspected for wholesomeness.

Bacon, except for slab style, doesn't keep well for longer than a week or 10 days. What happens? It begins to lose its lovely smoke flavor from the time it is sliced. At the end of a week or 10 days, it has very little flavor. At the end of 3 weeks, it frequently develops an off flavor. Of course if bacon isn't refrigerated, it will lose smoke flavor and develop off flavors much sooner.

What will you do if you're going camping? Either plan to buy bacon every week as you travel or buy it slab style.

At home, buy the amount that you plan to use during one week. If you have some left over, maybe some of the following recipes will help you to avoid waste.

Freezing

This is a waste of space because bacon loses flavor just as quickly in the freezer as in the refrigerator.

To cook bacon

Remove the number of slices desired in one piece with a spatula. As the bacon cooks, it will be easy to separate without tearing.

Get used to using meat tongs to handle bacon (and all meats). It is the safest way.

Naturally, the thinner the bacon the faster it will cook.

Frying

Place bacon in cold skillet and fry slowly. It is neither necessary nor desirable to pour off fat as it accumulates. It is too easy to burn oneself. Turn the bacon frequently and drain cooked bacon on absorbent paper. If it's cooked long enough, the bacon will be crisp.

Broiling

This is a quick easy way but stay alert or it will burn before you realize it. Place cold bacon in the bottom of the broiler pan. (You can save yourself scrubbing time if you line the pan with foil.) Place the pan 4 to 6 inches from the source of heat. Depending upon the temperature of the broiler, the way you like your bacon and the thickness of the bacon, the approximate time will be 2 to 6 minutes. Check often so it won't burn.

Baking

Put bacon in a large enough pan so it won't overlap. Preheat oven to 400°. Put bacon in oven. In a few minutes, separate slices. Bake approximately 5 minutes on each side or to the degree of doneness that you and your family prefer. Drain on absorbent paper and serve *hot.*

Bacon Curls: Stick one end of bacon between the tines of a fork while cooked bacon is still pliable. Twirl it around the fork and place it on absorbent paper. You have to move fast with this.

Leftover Bacon: Crumble leftover bacon and use it in salads, sandwiches, vegetables and sauces.

Drippings: Strain and store drippings, covered, in the refrigerator to use for seasoning and in gravies and sauces.

bacon and rye balls

1 pound bacon
1 package (8 oz.) cream cheese
1/4 cup evaporated milk or light cream
1 cup fine rye bread crumbs
1 teaspoon finely chopped onion
1 teaspoon Worcestershire sauce
1/2 cup chopped parsley

Cook bacon until crisp. Drain and chop into small pieces. Combine all ingredients except parsley. Chill for 2 hours. Shape into balls about 1 inch in diameter. Roll in parsley. Serve on picks. Yield: 20 balls or, if made into a spread, 1-1/2 cups.

snappy bacon dip

1 pound bacon
1 cup sour cream
1/2 cup catsup
1-1/2 teaspoons dry mustard
1/8 teaspoon ginger
1 package (3 oz.) cream cheese

Cook bacon and crumble very fine. Mix all ingredients. Chill in the refrigerator for at least three hours. Serve with corn chips or Ry-Krisp. Yield: 2-3/4 cups.

bacon onion broil

1 pound thin or regular sliced bacon
1 can (16 oz.) whole onions

Cut slices of bacon in half. Wrap each onion with 1/2 slice bacon. Secure with a pick. Place on broiler rack 4 inches from the source of heat. Broil about 7 minutes on the first side, turn and broil 4 minutes or until bacon is crisp. Serve immediately. Yield: About 16 whole onions with bacon.

quick
pea soup

4 thick or 6 thin slices bacon
1/2 cup chopped onion
1/2 cup finely chopped celery
2 cans (16 oz. each) peas
1 teaspoon chopped parsley
1 teaspoon salt
1/2 teaspoon freshly ground pepper
1 teaspoon dill weed (optional)
1 cup hot water

Cut bacon into 1/4-inch strips. Fry to a light brown. Add onion and celery. Cook until celery is almost tender. Add liquid from peas. Puree peas and add to mixture. Add other ingredients. Cover and simmer for 30 minutes. Yield: 1-1/2 qts.

NOTE: Increase this recipe and serve in a tureen as the, "one for the road", or the warmer upper after the game. It's pretty, tasty, hearty and can be made and frozen or refrigerated.

LUNCHEON MENU: Quick Pea Soup, Open Face Cheese Sandwiches, Tossed Green Salad, Prune or Apricot Whip, Beverage.

GARNISH: Float small cheese crackers or some dill weed on top.

colorful
coleslaw
with tangy
bacon
dressing

8 slices bacon
1/4 cup finely chopped onion
1 teaspoon salt
1 teaspoon sugar
1 teaspoon celery seed
2 tablespoons vinegar
1/4 cup mayonnaise
2 cups shredded cabbage
1/4 cup chopped pimiento
1/4 cup finely chopped green pepper

Cut bacon into 1/2-inch pieces. Cook with onion in a heavy skillet. Drain off half of drippings. Add salt, sugar, celery seed, vinegar and mayonnaise to bacon. Stir together. Combine cabbage, pimiento and green pepper. Add bacon dressing. Serve at once or chill and serve cold. Yield: 4 servings.

MENU: Fresh Mushroom Omelet, Frenched Green Beans, Sliced Tomatoes, Colorful Coleslaw With Tangy Bacon Dressing, Spice Cake With Broiled Coconut Frosting, Beverage.

bacon dressing for vegetables

1/4 pound bacon
1 tablespoon minced onion
2/3 cup tomato juice
1 tablespoon vinegar
1/4 teaspoon whole celery seed
Salt and pepper

Cut bacon into 1-inch strips. Brown in skillet. Remove bacon and add to cooked vegetables that are being kept hot. Drain all but 2 tablespoons of fat from skillet and save for other cooking purposes. Add onion to skillet and cook over low heat til tender. Add remaining ingredients and simmer for 5 minutes. Pour over hot vegetables. Yield: about 1 cup.

pennsylvania dutch spinach

10 slices bacon
1 pound fresh spinach
1/4 cup vinegar
1/4 cup water
1 hard cooked egg

Cut bacon into small pieces and cook until crisp. Wash spinach and cook rapidly in water that clings to the leaves. Pour off all but 2 tablespoons of bacon drippings. Dilute vinegar with water. Just before serving, add vinegar mixture to bacon drippings and combine with spinach. Garnish with hard cooked egg and serve immediately. Yield: 4 servings.

MENU: Beef Pot Roast, Pennsylvania Dutch Spinach, Buttered Noodles, Pineapple and Cottage Cheese Salad, Butter Brickle Ice Cream, Beverage.

GARNISH: Put pot roast on a large platter with noodles around it. Sprinkle noodles with paprika.

potato salad with bacon dressing

Bacon Dressing:

6 slices bacon
1 tablespoon flour
1/2 cup milk
1 egg
1/2 teaspoon prepared mustard
3/4 teaspoon salt
1 tablespoon sugar
1/4 teaspoon paprika
3 tablespoons vinegar
3 tablespoons water

Salad Ingredients:

1 quart cooked cubed potatoes (about 6 medium)
2 hard cooked eggs, diced
1/2 cup minced onion
1/2 cup diced sweet pickles
1 cup diced celery
2 teaspoons salt

Fry bacon until crisp. Drain on absorbent paper. Pour off all but 2 tablespoons in skillet. Add flour and blend until smooth. Combine milk and egg. Beat together. Mix in mustard, salt, sugar and paprika. Add to flour mixture. Stir over low heat until sauce thickens. Remove from heat. Slowly add vinegar and water together. Add chopped bacon to dressing. Cool. Combine salad ingredients. Mix in dressing. Cover and refrigerate for several hours to blend flavors. Yield: 6 to 7 cups.

MENU: Fried Chicken, Potato Salad With Bacon Dressing, Green Beans with Marjoram, Sliced Tomatoes with Fresh Dill, Sliced Cantaloupe, Beverage.

GARNISH: Use carrot curls and fresh dill or marjoram.

bacon and sweet-sour cabbage

4 cups shredded cabbage
1 pound bacon
3 tablespoons sugar
2 tablespoons flour
1 cup coarsely chopped onion
1/2 cup water
1/3 cup vinegar
1/4 teaspoon salt

Boil cabbage 5 minutes in a small amount of water in a covered saucepan. Drain. Cut bacon into crosswise strips. Fry until crisp. Drain on absorbent paper. Pour off all but 1/4 cup drippings. Add sugar and flour to drippings. Blend. Add onion, water, vinegar and salt. Cook and stir. After mixture thickens, cook 5 minutes to blend flavors. Add chopped bacon and cabbage. Heat 5 minutes or until cabbage and bacon are hot. Yield: 4 servings.

MENU: Bacon and Sweet-Sour Cabbage, Buttered Brown Rice, Mixed Vegetables, Sunshine Salad, Chocolate Cake, Beverage.

GARNISH: Cherry Tomatoes.

barbecued bacon luncheon salad

2 tablespoons lemon juice
1/2 teaspoon dried basil
1/2 cup barbecue sauce
2 tablespoons mayonnaise
1 medium head of lettuce
1 large tomato
1 pound sliced bacon
1-1/2 cups diced celery
2 hard cooked eggs

Heat lemon juice and basil to boiling and cool. Mix with barbecue sauce and mayonnaise. Chill. Remove 4 cups from head of lettuce. Cut the rest into small pieces. Peel tomato and cut into 8 pieces. Chill well. Cut bacon into 1/2 inch strips and fry til crisp. Drain. Combine all ingredients. Serve immediately. Yield: 4 servings.

MENU: Barbecued Bacon Luncheon Salad, Carrot Sticks, Shoestring Potatoes, Fresh Fruit Shortcake, Beverage.

GARNISH: None needed.

tomato aspic with bacon mayonnaise

2 tablespoons unflavored gelatin
4 cups vegetable cocktail juice
1/8 teaspoon dried basil
1 pound sliced bacon
1 cup mayonnaise
2 tablespoons lemon juice

Soften gelatin in 1/2 cup vegetable cocktail juice. Add basil to remaining juice. Cover and boil for 5 minutes. Strain. Add gelatin mixture to hot juice. Stir til dissolved. Pour into an 8-inch ring mold that has been rinsed in cold water. Place in refrigerator until set. Just before serving cut bacon into 1/2-inch pieces. Fry until crisp. Drain. Combine mayonnaise and lemon juice. Add bacon. Unmold. Serve with bacon mayonnaise dressing. Yield: 6 servings.

MENU: Broiled Lamb Shoulder Chops, Potato Puffs, Minted Baby Carrots, Tomato Aspic with Bacon Mayonnaise, Apricot Pie a la Mode, Beverage.

GARNISH: Garnish chops with the carrots and fresh mint.

bacon and stewed tomatoes

1/2 pound sliced bacon
4 large tomatoes
1/4 cup water
1-1/2 teaspoons onion juice
1/4 teaspoon dried basil
1/2 cup chopped celery
1 teaspoon sugar
1 teaspoon salt
1/8 teaspoon pepper
1 tablespoon cornmeal

Cut bacon into small crosswise strips. Fry til crisp. Drain and save 2 tablespoons drippings. Peel tomatoes. Cut each into 8 pieces. Put tomatoes, water, onion juice, basil, celery, sugar, salt, pepper and bacon drippings in a saucepan and cook, covered, slowly for 25 minutes until celery is tender. Add cornmeal. Stir and heat til thickened. Add bacon and serve immediately. Yield: 4 servings.

MENU: Fish Sticks, Bacon and Stewed Tomatoes, Buttered Green Peas, French Fried Potatoes, Cucumber and Green Pepper Rings, Chilled Fresh Pineapple, Beverage.

GARNISH: Green Pepper Rings.

bacon herb rice with quick cheese sauce

1 pound sliced bacon
1/4 cup finely chopped onion
1/2 cup uncooked rice
1-1/2 cups water
1/4 cup each, finely chopped parsley and celery leaves
1/4 teaspoon each dried marjoram and thyme

Cut bacon into 1/2-inch pieces. Fry in a heavy skillet until browned and crisp. Remove bacon from skillet. Drain on absorbent paper. Pour off all but 2 tablespoons drippings. Add onion and brown. Add rice, water and seasonings. Cover and cook slowly for 25 minutes or until rice is tender and moisture is gone. Add bacon. Serve with cheese sauce.

Cheese Sauce

1/2 pound shredded cheddar cheese
1/2 cup milk
1/8 teaspoon garlic salt

Combine all ingredients. Cook slowly for 5 minutes or until cheese is melted. Serve over Bacon Herb Rice. Yield: 4 servings.

MENU: Bacon Herb Rice With Quick Cheese Sauce, Buttered Asparagus, Crisp Garden Salad, Fresh Fruit, Beverage.

GARNISH: Pickled Fruit.

special baked beans

8 slices of bacon
2 cans (16 oz. each) baked beans
1/4 cup chopped onion
1/2 cup brown sugar, firmly packed
1 tablespoon prepared mustard
1 tablespoon vinegar
1 teaspoon Worcestershire sauce
1/4 teaspoon salt

Cut 6 slices of bacon into small pieces and fry. Drain. Add to the other ingredients. Put in a casserole. Cut the other two slices of bacon in half. Put on top of beans. Heat for 1 hour in a preheated 375° oven. Yield: 4 servings.

MENU: Special Baked Beans, Buttered Broccoli, Fried Apples, Pickled Beets and Hard Cooked Eggs, Corn Bread, Cookies, Beverage.

GARNISH: None needed.

bacon and ground beef filets

8 to 10 slices bacon
2 pounds ground beef
1/4 cup chopped onion
1 egg, beaten
1 cup shredded cheddar cheese
3 tablespoons tangy catsup
3 tablespoons Worcestershire sauce
1 teaspoon seasoned salt
1/2 teaspoon pepper

Place bacon on a board, side touching side. Combine all other ingredients. Press and roll meat mixture into a 10-inch roll. Place the meat roll on the bacon. Draw the strips around the meat. Fasten with picks. Slice in 1-inch rounds so that a slice of bacon surrounds each slice of meat. Broil about 5 minutes on each side. Yield: 8 to 10 servings.

MENU: Bacon and Ground Beef Filets, French Fried Onion Rings, Corn O'Brien, Herbed Tomatoes, Sour Dough Bread, Fresh Fruit, Beverage.

GARNISH: Herbed Tomato Slices.

quick broiled sandwiches

4 slices bread
2 medium tomatoes
4 slices bacon
1 cup shredded cheddar cheese
3 tablespoons chopped green pepper
3 tablespoons chopped onion
Cayenne Pepper

Toast bread on one side. Peel tomatoes. Place two slices of tomato on the untoasted side of each slice of bread. Sprinkle equal amounts of cheese, green pepper and onion on top of the tomatoes. Cut bacon crosswise into 1/4-inch pieces. Put equal amounts on each sandwich. Add a dash of Cayenne pepper. Broil sandwiches 4 inches from the source of heat for 3 to 5 minutes, until the bacon is cooked and the cheese is melted. Yield: 4 servings.

MENU: This is the kind of sandwich that goes with whatever happens to be in the refrigerator, like a glass of milk and some fresh fruit.

quick bacon sandwiches

8 slices bacon
1 can (10-1/2 oz.) cream of celery soup
2 medium tomatoes
1/2 teaspoon dry mustard
4 slices hot buttered toast

Fry bacon and drain. Combine soup and mustard. Heat to boiling. Peel and slice tomatoes. Put slices on toast. Top with two slices of bacon and spoon hot soup over sandwich. Yield: 4 servings.

MENU: Quick Bacon Sandwiches, Potato Salad, Relish Tray, Gingerbread, Beverage.

GARNISH: Sprinkle paprika on top of sandwiches.

tasty ranch style bacon sandwiches

8 slices bacon
8 slices buttered toast
1 can (16 oz.) baked beans
1 cup shredded cheddar cheese

Cut bacon slices in half crosswise. Cover each slice of toast with 1/4 cup beans. Top with cheese. Put 2 pieces of bacon on top of each sandwich. Broil about 5 inches from the source of heat for 5 minutes or until bacon is crisp.

MENU: Vegetable Soup, Tasty Ranch Style Bacon Sandwiches, Dill Pickles, Apples, Beverage.

GARNISH: Pickles

bacon chop suey

1 pound bacon, sliced
1/4 cup sliced onion
2 cups diced celery
1 can (4 oz.) mushrooms and liquid
1-1/2 cups water
1/4 teaspoon pepper
2 tablespoons soy sauce
2 teaspoons cornstarch

Cut bacon slices in half and cook until crisp. Drain, save 2 tablespoons drippings. Cook onions and celery in drippings until tender. Add mushrooms and liquid, water, pepper and soy sauce. Cover and simmer 20 minutes. Mix cornstarch with small amount of cold water. Add to mixture. Cook and stir til thickened. Add bacon. Serve hot. Yield: 4 servings.

MENU: Bacon Chop Suey, Hot Rice, Chop Suey Noodles, Chinese Cabbage, Thousand Island Dressing, Almond Cookies, Beverage.

GARNISH: Pimiento Strips

bacon and cheese specials

6 frank buns, split
1 jar (5 oz.) sharp-flavored cheese
1 tablespoon finely chopped onion
2 medium tomatoes
12 slices bacon

Toast buns lightly. Combine cheese and onion. Peel tomatoes. Cut into 1/4 inch slices. Cut slices in half. Put tomatoes on 6 bun halves. Spread cheese mixture over tomatoes. Place on rack and broil 3 inches from the source of heat until cheese is lightly browned. Remove from the broiler. Broil bacon til crisp. Drain on absorbent paper. Put bacon on cheese and bun top on bacon. Yield: 6 sandwiches.

MENU: Bean Soup, Bacon and Cheese Specials, Carrot and Celery Sticks, Fresh Fruit, Beverage.

GARNISH: None needed

our favorite spaghetti

1 pound bacon, sliced
1 cup chopped onion
1/2 cup chopped green pepper
1 can (16 oz.) tomatoes
1-1/2 teaspoons salt
2 teaspoons chili powder
1 teaspoon paprika
4 cups cooked spaghetti (8 oz. pkg.)
1 cup shredded cheddar cheese

Cut all but 5 slices bacon into 1/2-inch pieces. Cook bacon pieces slowly until lightly browned. Add onion and green pepper. Cook until tender. Drain. Combine with tomatoes, salt, chili powder, paprika and spaghetti. Place in a buttered baking dish and spread cheese on top. Cover with 5 strips of bacon. Bake in a preheated 350° oven for 45 minutes or until cheese has melted. To make bacon more crisp, if necessary, place under the broiler for a few minutes. Yield: 6 servings.

MENU: Our Favorite Spaghetti, Franks, Green Salad, Toasted Hard Rolls, Fresh Fruit Sundaes, Beverage.

GARNISH: Sliced Stuffed olives sprinkled on top of the spaghetti.

bacon supper skillet

1 pound sliced bacon
1 medium onion, chopped
1 can (16 oz.) whole kernel yellow corn
1 can (10-1/2 oz.) green pea soup
1/2 teaspoon dill weed
1/2 teaspoon curry powder

Cut bacon into 1/2-inch strips. Fry until almost crisp. Add onion and cook til tender. Drain and save drippings. Combine soup, corn, dill, curry powder and 2 tablespoons drippings in skillet. Heat til hot. Add corn liquid, if necessary. Top with bacon. Yield: 4 servings.

MENU: Bacon Supper Skillet, Buttered Asparagus, Sliced Tomatoes And Cottage Cheese, Sunshine Cake, Beverage.

GARNISH: Tiny red and yellow pickled peppers.

snappy broiled sandwiches

5 slices bacon
6 slices bread
1 cup shredded sharp cheddar cheese
2 tablespoons finely chopped onion
1/4 cup chopped stuffed olives
2 tablespoons mayonnaise
1 teaspoon Worcestershire sauce
1/2 teaspoon chili powder

Toast bread on one side in broiler. Mix all ingredients except bread and bacon. Spread cheese on untoasted side of bread. Cut bacon into small pieces. Sprinkle on sandwiches. Broil until cheese is bubbling and bacon is crisp. Yield: 6 servings. NOTE: Cut these into tiny pieces and serve as appetizers.

MENU: Snappy Broiled Sandwiches, Crisp Green Salad, Baked Apples, Beverage.

GARNISH: Sliced Sweet Pickle.

bacon and oats muffins

1/2 pound sliced bacon
3 tablespoons salad oil
1-1/4 cups milk, scalded
3/4 cup quick cooking oats
1 egg, beaten
1-1/2 cups sifted flour
3 tablespoons sugar
4 teaspoons baking powder
1/2 teaspoon salt

Chop bacon and fry til crisp. Drain. Pour salad oil and milk over oats. Let stand 15 minutes. Beat in egg. Sift together the dry ingredients. Stir bacon and liquid mixture into dry ingredients. Mix just enough to moisten flour mixture. Fill buttered muffin tins 2/3 full. Bake in a preheated 425° oven for 15 to 20 minutes until muffins are browned. Remove from pans immediately to keep muffins from getting soggy. Yield: 12 medium or 16 small muffins. NOTE: These muffins can be frozen and reheated in the foil package in a 325° oven for 15 to 20 minutes or until hot. This is a good way to serve hot breads for breakfast without having to get up in the middle of the night.

MENU: Fresh Orange Juice, Fried Eggs, Bacon and Oats Muffins, Red Raspberry Jam, Coffee, Milk.

GARNISH: Serve tiny sprigs of mint leaves in orange juice.

bacon pineapple wheels

8 slices pineapple
Ground cinnamon
8 slices bacon

Sprinkle pineapple with cinnamon. Cut bacon in half lengthwise Wrap two strips through center and around each pineapple slice pinwheel style. Secure with picks. Be careful not to stretch bacon or it will shrink and tear when broiling. Broil for 3 to 4 minutes on each side until bacon is cooked. Remove picks before serving. Yield: 4 servings.

MENU: Fresh Strawberries, Breakfast Omelets, Bacon Pineapple Wheels, Bran Muffins, Orange Marmalade, Coffee, Milk.

GARNISH: A sprig of green is all that's necessary and just hope that the men don't object too much.

hearty breakfast dish

4 slices bacon
2 cups cooked cubed potatoes (about 3 medium)
4 eggs, beaten
1 teaspoon salt
Fresh ground pepper

Cut bacon into 1/2-inch strips and brown slowly in a skillet. Add potatoes and brown lightly. Season eggs. Pour over bacon and potatoes. Stir slowly over low heat until the eggs are set. Yield: 4 servings. Serve extra bacon on the side. NOTE: For a luncheon dish, add 3 tablespoons of minced onion while the potatoes and bacon are browning.

MENU: Cantaloupe, Hearty Breakfast Dish, Whole Spiced Crab Apple, Toasted English Muffins, Honeybutter, Beverage.

GARNISH: None necessary.

bacon bundles with cheese sauce

1 can (16 oz.) Asparagus Spears
8 slices Bacon

Divide asparagus into 8 small bundles. Wrap a strip of bacon around each and secure with a pick. Broil until bacon is crisp. Remove picks and serve with cheese sauce. Yield: 4 servings. NOTE: Cooked whole carrots or green beans can be substituted for asparagus. Naturally, fresh cooked asparagus would be the best if in season.

Cheese Sauce

2 tablespoons butter
2 tablespoons flour
1 cup shredded cheddar cheese
1 cup milk
1/2 teaspoon salt
Cayenne pepper

Melt butter and stir in flour. Gradually stir in milk and cook and stir until thick and to the boiling point. Cool slightly and stir in cheese. Heat and stir til cheese melts. Serve over Bacon Bundles. NOTE: Mixture is cooled to below the boiling point to prevent cheese from stringing. Yield: 1-1/2 cups.

MENU: Bacon Bundles With Cheese Sauce, Sauteed Cherry Tomatoes, Cauliflower Amandine, Sunshine Salad, Sponge Cake Nests Filled with Ice Cream and Butterscotch Sauce, Beverage.

GARNISH: None needed.

baked potatoes supreme

4 baked potatoes
1/2 pound sliced bacon
1/2 teaspoon salt
1 tablespoon butter
2 tablespoons cream

Scrub potatoes and grease lightly. Bake in a preheated 400° oven until soft in center, about 40 minutes. (If you're cooking a roast, the potatoes will cook just fine in a 325° oven, they will just cook a little longer.) Cut bacon into pieces and cook til crisp. Drain. Scoop out the inside of the potato and mix it with hot mixture of salt, butter and cream. Beat til fluffy. Stir in bacon. Refill potatoes. Put in the broiler to brown. Yield: 4 servings.

MENU: Glazed Pork Roast, Baked Potatoes Supreme, Sour Cream, Herbed Carrots, Sweet Sour Sliced Tomatoes, Warm Cherry Pie a la Mode, Beverage.

GARNISH: Currant Flavored Meringue Pears With Greens.

Meringue pears

1 egg white
1/4 teaspoon salt
1/2 cup currant jelly
12 canned pear halves

Beat egg white until stiff. Add salt and jelly. Beat until meringue is thick and forms peaks. Spread on cut surface of each pear half. Place in preheated 375° oven for 5 minutes. Turn off and leave pears in the oven for 10 minutes or until the peaks are browned. NOTE: any flavor of tart jelly can be used.

salt pork

This is a meat that was eaten by the early settlers because it kept well without the refrigeration that they didn't have. It is still eaten and loved by many people all over the country. My Grandmother taught me to eat it.

Buy it by the piece; a pound will usually make 6 ample servings. Select what is known as the "streaky" pieces. These have the most lean streaks through them. Slice the meat about 1/4 inch thick and pour boiling water over it to remove excess salt. Dip in cornmeal and fry til crisp. Make a cream gravy with the drippings, flour and milk.

Salt Pork is also excellent to use for seasoning most vegetables including baked beans.

smoked jowls

This is also salt pork that is used for seasoning vegetables. It is square in shape while the salt pork is the same shape as bacon but isn't quite as salty. This is sometimes called seasoning bacon.

pork sausage

Generally, pure pork sausage is available in any or all of the following styles.

link sausage

The natural casing takes longer to cook and has more shrinkage but it does add more seasoning if some other food is cooked with it. Some say it is juicier. It is also cheaper to purchase. However, don't forget to consider the shrink when comparing the overall cost.

The skinless precooked pork sausage need only be reheated. Since the initial shrinkage has occured when cooked by the processor, this sausage is not as satisfactory for cooking with other foods. It is more expensive to purchase but consider the lack of shrink. You'll have to be the judge.

roll or bulk pork sausage

This is sold by the pound in branded packages or as a specialty by your meat dealer in the quantities you wish. Many a meat dealer has made his reputation on his special pork sausage. Packers' branded sausage is frequently available in mild, medium or hot seasoning so be sure to read the label.

smoked pork sausage

Smoked Country Sausage is available in the large continuous link or in the frankfurter-size link. It is usually coarsely chopped and the amount of smoke varies with the processor.

Precooked skinless smoked sausage links are usually the size of regular sausage links.

Storing

Keep pork sausage very cold. Either freeze it or use it within three days.

Freezing

Because sausage is ground meat and because it has a high fat content, it is best not to keep it in the freezer for longer than a month for best flavor. The smoked sausage shouldn't be kept longer than a week. Like bacon, why bother? It will keep just as well in the refrigerator.

Cooking

Always follow the packer's directions when you first try a product. Then, if you have other preferences, you will know how to apply them to the product. In general, the links with casings are steamed for five minutes and then fried or baked. The roll pork sausages are cooked by frying or baking. The skinless are reheated any way you please because they are already cooked.

link pork sausage

TO FRY: Place in a cold skillet, add 1/4 cup water and cover. Cook slowly for 5 minutes. Remove cover, pour off water and brown slowly. Handle with tongs so the casings won't be pricked.

TO BAKE: Place links in a shallow pan. Bake in a preheated 400° oven for 20 to 30 minutes. Turn once or twice during the baking process.

Be sure there is no pink showing in the sausage when it is finished cooking.

roll or bulk pork sausage

Cut the sausage into slices about 1/2 inch thick. Place in a cold skillet or in a preheated 400° oven and cook until the patties are brown and not pink on the inside. It should take about 15 minutes on the surface of the range and about 20 to 25 minutes in the oven. The oven method is excellent when you want to cook a large quantity. Keep an eye on it, however, because the time will vary depending on the number of patties that you are cooking and how close together they are.

smoked pork sausage

In general, cook them like regular link sausage. Cut the rope or long link into pieces about 4 inches long and proceed just as with the links. If there are label instructions, always follow them at least the first time.

sausage dressing casserole

1 pound pork sausage links
1 egg
1/2 cup milk
3-1/2 cups bread crumbs
2 tablespoons chopped onion
2 tablespoons chopped parsley
1/2 cup chopped celery
1 teaspoon salt

Put links in a cold skillet. Add 1/4 cup water, cover and cook over low heat for 5 minutes. Pour off water and brown lightly. Drain off fat. Add egg to milk. Mix. Combine with bread crumbs, onion, parsley, celery and salt. Pour into greased shallow baking dish (10 x 6 x 2). Put sausage on top of dressing. Use sausage drippings, 2 tablespoons flour, 1/4 teaspoon salt and 1 cup milk to make gravy to serve over dressing. Yield: 4 servings.

MENU: Sausage Dressing Casserole, Pickled Carrots, Tossed Green Salad, Custard Pie, Beverage.

GARNISH: Pickled Carrots with Parsley tops.

sausage links and raisin sauce

1 pound link pork sausage
1 cup water
2 tablespoons seedless raisins
1/8 teaspoon salt
1/4 cup finely chopped green pepper
1 teaspoon cornstarch
2 tablespoons sugar
2 tablespoons vinegar.

Simmer sausage for 5 minutes in 1/4 cup water in a covered skillet. Drain off drippings. Add 1/4 cup water, raisins, salt and green pepper. Cover pan and cook 5 minutes. Mix cornstarch and sugar. Slowly stir in remaining water and vinegar. Add to sausage. Cover and simmer 20 minutes or until thickened. Stir occasionally. Serve hot. Yield: 4 servings.

MENU: Sausage Links and Raisin Sauce, Fluffy Rice, Winter Squash, mashed, Sunshine Salad, Chocolate Pudding, Beverage.

GARNISH: None needed.

sausage and corn bake

1 pound link pork sausage
1 can (16 oz.) yellow whole kernel corn, drained
1 can (10-1/2 oz.) cream of asparagus soup
2 tablespoons finely chopped onion
1/2 teaspoon dill seed
1/8 teaspoon pepper

Steam sausage for 5 minutes in a heavy skillet. Combine remaining ingredients. Pour mixture into a greased baking dish. Top with sausage. Bake in a preheated 400° oven for 30 minutes or until sausage is brown. Yield: 4 servings.

MENU: Sausage and Corn Bake, Pennsylvania Dutch Spinach, Boiled Potatoes, Waldorf Salad, Coffee Ice Cream, Beverage.

GARNISH: Sliced Stuffed Olives.

scalloped cabbage and sausage

1 pound pork sausage links
1 medium head cabbage
3 teaspoons flour
1-1/2 cups milk
1/2 cup shredded cheddar cheese

Steam links for five minutes. Drain off water and brown slightly. Save drippings. Cut cabbage into wedges and cook in boiling water until tender. Drain. Measure 3 tablespoons drippings back into the skillet. Add flour and blend. Stir in milk and cook until sauce thickens. Stir constantly. Place cabbage in a greased casserole. Pour on sauce. Top with sausage. Sprinkle with cheese. Bake in a preheated 350° oven for 40 minutes. Yield: 4 servings.

MENU: Scalloped Cabbage and Sausage, Baked Potatoes, Sauteed Zucchini, Pineapple and Cottage Salad, Date Pudding, Beverage.

GARNISH: Pimiento pieces.

snappy sausage and applesauce casserole

1 pound link pork sausage
2 cups cooked noodles (1 cup uncooked)
2 tablespoons sausage drippings
1 can (16 oz.) applesauce
3 tablespoons lemon juice
1/4 teaspoon nutmeg

Steam and pan fry sausages until lightly browned. Drain drippings. Mix noodles with drippings, applesauce, juice, and nutmeg. Place mixture in a greased 1-1/2-quart casserole. Top with sausage. Bake in a preheated 350° oven for 20 minutes or until bubbling hot. Yield: 4 servings.

MENU: Snappy Sausage and Applesauce Casserole, Buttered Corn, Green Peas, Perfection Salad, Butterscotch Pudding, Beverage.

GARNISH: None needed.

spaghetti sausage bake

1 pound link pork sausage
2 tablespoons flour
1 cup milk
1/2 teaspoon salt
1/4 teaspoon pepper
1/2 cup crumbled blue cheese
2 cans (15-1/2 oz. each) spaghetti with tomato sauce (3-1/2 cups)
1/4 cup chopped stuffed olives

Steam and fry sausage until lightly browned. Drain on absorbent paper. Remove all but 2 tablespoons drippings from skillet. Stir in flour. Add milk and stir constantly until thickened. Add salt, pepper and cheese. Stir until cheese melts. Add spaghetti, green pepper and olives. Pour into a greased 2-quart casserole. Top with sausage. Bake in a preheated 350° oven for 30 minutes or until browned. Yield: 4 servings.

MENU: Spaghetti Sausage Bake, Buttered Broccoli, Glazed Carrots, Molded Cranberry Relish Salad, Brownies, Beverage.

GARNISH: The links garnish the spaghetti but if you want to be fancier, use sliced, stuffed olives or peeled cherry tomatoes.

sweet-sour sausage

1 pound link pork sausage
1/2 cup chopped onion
2 tablespoons salad oil
1 chicken bouillon cube
1/4 cup boiling water
1/2 cup vinegar

1/2 cup sugar
2 teaspoons kitchen bouquet
1/8 teaspoon ginger
2 teaspoons cornstarch
1/4 teaspoon salt
1 can (16 oz.) green beans

Steam and brown sausage. Drain most of fat. Brown onions. Add bouillon cube and water to onion. Cover and cook slowly for 10 minutes. Combine vinegar, sugar, kitchen bouquet, ginger, cornstarch and salt. Stir into onion mixture. Cook slowly, stirring constantly until thick. Add green beans and cook for 10 minutes or until flavors are blended. Pour over sausage and serve hot. Yield: 4 servings.

MENU: Sweet-Sour Sausage, Buttered Noodles, Carrot and Raisin Salad, Hard Rolls, Apple Crisp, Beverage.

GARNISH: Some snipped pieces of pimiento will add the right contrast.

tempting sausage with caraway seed

1 pound link pork sausage
1 cup uncooked elbow macaroni, cooked
1/4 cup finely chopped onion
1 can (10-1/2 oz.) cream of celery soup
1 teaspoon caraway seed
1/2 teaspoon dry mustard

Steam and brown sausage lightly. Combine the rest of ingredients. Place 1/2 of sausage in the bottom of a buttered 1-quart casserole. Pour in macaroni mixture. Top with remaining sausage. Bake in a preheated 350° oven for 40 minutes or until brown and bubbling. Yield: 4 servings.

MENU: Tempting Sausage With Caraway Seed, Buttered Spinach, Baby Lima Beans, Molded Fruit Salad, Coconut Layer Cake, Beverage.

GARNISH: None needed.

american casserole

1 pound pork sausage links
1/4 cup water
2/3 cup shredded cheddar cheese
3/4 cup concentrated tomato soup
1 can (16 oz.) hominy, drained
1/4 teaspoon seasoned salt
2 tablespoons chopped green pepper

Steam and partially brown sausage. Drain. Combine remaining ingredients and pour into a greased 1-1/2-quart casserole dish. Top with sausage links. Bake in a preheated 350° oven about 25 minutes or until brown and bubbly. Yield: 4 servings.

MENU: American Casserole, Sliced Beets in Orange Sauce, Green Salad, Pumpkin Chiffon Pie, Beverage.

GARNISH: None needed.

colorful sausage casserole

1 can (16 oz.) whole kernel corn, drained
2 eggs, beaten
1 cup milk
1 teaspoon salt
1/8 teaspoon pepper
2 tablespoons chopped green pepper
1 pound pork sausage links

Combine corn, eggs, milk, seasonings and green pepper. Place in a buttered casserole. Bake in a preheated 350° oven for 20 minutes. Steam and lightly brown sausage. After the casserole has been in the oven for 20 minutes, place sausage on the corn mixture and continue baking until mixture is set and sausage is thoroughly cooked. Total baking time: about 1 hour. Yield: 4 servings.

MENU: Colorful Sausage Casserole, Stewed Tomatoes, Cabbage Slaw, Plum Cobbler, Beverage.

GARNISH: None needed.

glazed sausages and apples

1 pound link pork sausage
8 slices tart apple 1/2 inch thick
1/2 cup orange juice
2 tablespoons grated orange peel
1/2 cup honey
1/4 teaspoon cinnamon

Steam and lightly brown sausage. Place apple slices in skillet. Mix orange juice and peel, honey and cinnamon. Pour over apples and sausage. Cover and cook slowly for 8 minutes or until apples are tender. Place 2 sausage links on the top of each apple slice. Yield: 4 servings.

MENU: Glazed Sausages and Apples, Green Peas, Brown Rice, Wilted Lettuce Salad, Chocolate Cake, Beverage.

GARNISH: Serve the peas on the same platter with the apples.

harvest casserole

1 pound pork sausage links
2 tablespoons chopped onion
1 can (10-1/2 oz.) cream of tomato soup
1 small package (5 oz.) noodles, cooked
1/2 cup shredded cheddar cheese

Steam and pan fry sausage until lightly browned. Remove from skillet and brown onion. Drain and save drippings. Combine onion, tomato soup, noodles and 1/4 cup drippings. Put in a buttered casserole, top with sausage and sprinkle with cheese. Bake uncovered in a preheated 350° oven for 30 minutes or until bubbly and brown. Yield: 4 servings.

MENU: Harvest Casserole, Green Peppers Stuffed With Corn, Dilled Carrots, Molded Pear Salad, Peach Shortcake, Beverage.

GARNISH: Not necessary.

sausage o'brien

1 pound link pork sausage
2 cups cooked diced potatoes
2 tablespoons minced green pepper
2 tablespoons minced pimiento
2 tablespoons minced onion

Steam and brown sausage links. Remove sausage from skillet. Keep hot. Brown potatoes, green pepper, pimiento and onion in 3 tablespoons of sausage drippings. Serve hot, topped with sausage. NOTE: For variety, substitute cooked hominy, lima beans or rice for the cooked potatoes. Yield: 4 servings.

MENU: Sausage O'Brien, Mixed Vegetables, Cabbage, Celery and Pineapple Salad, Banana Nut Cake, Beverage.

GARNISH: None needed.

spicy sausage skillet

1 pound pork sausage links
1 medium onion, sliced
1/2 cup chopped celery
2 tablespoons brown sugar
2 teaspoons mustard
1 tablespoon Worcestershire sauce
1 cup water
1/2 cup catsup
1 can (8 oz.) tomato puree
4 medium potatoes

Steam and brown sausage. When fat has gathered in skillet, add onion and celery. Cook 'til soft and yellow. Remove excess drippings from pan. Add all other ingredients except potatoes. Pare potatoes. Slice thin. Add to skillet. Cover and cook slowly until potatoes are tender—about an hour. If sauce gets too thick, add more water. Yield: 4 servings.

MENU: Spicy Sausage Skillet, Buttered Wax Beans, Green Salad, Butterscotch Sundaes With Salted Peanuts, Beverage.

GARNISH: Serve on a platter with a sprig or two of celery leaves.

sausage and hot potato salad

6 medium potatoes, boiled
1 pound pork sausage links
1/4 cup minced onion
1/2 cup vinegar
1/4 cup water
3/4 teaspoon salt
2 teaspoons sugar

Cube potatoes. Steam and brown sausage. Remove links from pan. Brown onions in drippings. Add vinegar, water, salt and sugar. Stir and boil for several minutes. Pour over potatoes. Arrange sausage links on top. Yield: 4 servings.

MENU: Sausage and Hot Potato Salad, Sliced Tomatoes, Buttered Crisp Carrots, Deep Dish Blueberry Pie, Beverage.

GARNISH: Green Pepper Rings.

link pork sausage omelet

1 pound link pork sausage
2 tablespoons butter or margarine
1 cup medium seasoned white sauce
4 eggs

Fry sausage over low heat to partially cook. Butter heavy skillet and place in the oven to get piping hot. Cook white sauce. Separate eggs and beat the yolks until thick and lemon colored. Add to white sauce and blend. Beat whites until stiff, but not dry. Fold into mixture. Pour omelet into hot pan. Place sausages on top. Cover and cook over low heat about 8 minutes or until omelet begins to puff. Uncover and put in a preheated 325° oven for 30 minutes or until firm on top. Serve immediately. Yield: 4 servings.

MENU: Link Pork Sausage Omelet, Sweet Sour Red Cabbage, Mixed Green Vegetables, Fresh Fruit, Beverage.

GARNISH: None needed.

sausage bean bake

1 pound link pork sausage
3 cups cooked dried lima beans
2 tablespoons molasses
1/3 cup catsup
1 cup cooking liquid from beans
1 teaspoon salt
1 teaspoon prepared mustard

Steam and brown sausage slowly. Place beans in a 1-1/2-quart casserole. Mix together molasses, catsup, liquid, salt and mustard. Pour over beans. Arrange sausage on top. Bake in a preheated 350° oven for 30 minutes. Yield: 4 servings.

MENU: Sausage-Bean Bake, Pennsylvania Dutch Spinach, Buttered Baby Beets, Carrot and Celery Salad, Angel Cake With Cherry Sauce, Beverage.

GARNISH: Put a daub of catsup in the center and arrange the sausage in spokes around it.

sausage surprises

1 pound link pork sausage
2 cups cooked mashed sweet potatoes
1 tablespoon sausage drippings
2 tablespoons brown sugar
1/2 teaspoon salt
1/2 teaspoon cinnamon
1/8 teaspoon white pepper
1/2 cup orange juice
8 orange slices, 1/2 inch thick
Corn Cereal

Steam and brown sausages slowly. Combine sweet potatoes, sausage drippings, brown sugar, salt, pepper and cinnamon. Add orange juice to make a stiff but moist sweet potato mixture. (Sweet potatoes vary in moisture so no definite amount can be given.) Put a spoonful of sweet potato mixture on each orange slice. Put two links on top of each slice. Cover with the remaining sweet potato mixture. Sprinkle with crushed corn cereal. Bake in a preheated 350° oven for 15 minutes or until hot. Yield: 4 servings.

MENU: Sausage Surprises, Buttered Cauliflower, Tossed Green Salad, Green Goddess Dressing, Spice Cup Cakes, Beverage.

GARNISH: Sprinkle cauliflower with paprika and serve around the surprises. A sprig or two of greens will do wonders for the platter.

hearty potato and sausage casserole

1 pound link pork sausage
1/4 cup chopped onion
2 tablespoons finely chopped green pepper
1 tablespoon flour
1-1/2 cups milk
1 teaspoon salt
6 small cooked potatoes, sliced thin

Fry sausage until lightly browned. Remove from skillet. Brown onion and green pepper. Put with sausage. Drain all but 2 tablespoons drippings. Stir in flour. Slowly stir in milk. Cook over low heat until thick. Add salt, pepper and onion. Place alternate layers of sliced potatoes and white sauce in a 2-quart casserole. Place sausage on top. Bake in a preheated 350° oven for 35 minutes. Yield: 4 servings.

MENU: Hearty Potato And Sausage Casserole, Buttered Green Beans, Grapefruit Salad, Apple Cobbler, Beverage.

GARNISH: Red and Yellow Pickled Peppers.

sausage and sauerkraut a la spareribs

1 pound roll pork sausage
1 pound sauerkraut

Form sausage into 8 thin patties. Brown them on both sides in the skillet on the surface of the range or in a 400° oven. Remove patties and drain skillet or pan. Place sauerkraut in the pan and mix with 2 tablespoons of drippings. Put patties on top. Put in a preheated 300° oven for 25 minutes or until the sauerkraut is thoroughly hot and there is no pink in the center of the sausage. Yield: 4 servings.

Variation: Some people like a little caraway or thyme mixed with the sauerkraut.

MENU: Sausage and Sauerkraut a la Spareribs, Boiled Potatoes, Glazed Carrots, Tomato Aspic With Cottage Cheese, Chocolate Cake, Beverage.

GARNISH: Sliced Stuffed Olives or parsley the potatoes.

sausage fondue

1 pound roll pork sausage
1 tablespoon butter
1 cup scalded milk
1 cup soft bread crumbs (3 to 4 slices)
1/4 teaspoon salt
4 eggs

Fry and crumble sausage to a light brown. Drain well. Add butter to milk, then pour over bread crumbs. Combine with salt and sausage. Separate eggs. Add egg yolks and beat thoroughly. Beat egg whites 'til stiff but not dry. Cut and fold into yolk mixture. Pour into 1-1/2-quart casserole. Bake in a preheated 325° oven for 45 minutes. Serve at once with cream gravy. Yield: 4 servings.

MENU: Sausage Fondue, Mixed Wild and Long Grain Rice, Green Beans and Sauteed Mushrooms, Tomato and Cucumber Salad, Blackberry Pie a la Mode, Beverage.

GARNISH: Greens.

spicy cabbage and sausage casserole

1/2 pound roll pork sausage
1 tablespoon wine vinegar
1 tablespoon paprika
1 cup hot water
6 soda crackers, crushed
4 cups shredded cabbage

Crumble and fry sausage thoroughly. Remove sausage from skillet and save 2 tablespoons drippings. Combine the 2 tablespoons drippings with vinegar, paprika and hot water. Combine sausage with cracker crumbs and sauce. Cook cabbage in salted boiling water about 7 minutes. Drain. Put a layer of cabbage in a 1-1/2-quart casserole. Top with a layer of sausage mixture and repeat. Bake uncovered in a preheated 350° oven for 30 minutes or until bubbly and brown. Yield: 6 servings.

MENU: Beef Pot Roast, Spicy Cabbage and Sausage Casserole, Buttered Corn, Molded Lime Salad With Pears and Cream Cheese, Black Walnut Sour Cream Cake, Beverage.

GARNISH: This needs something red. Sliced stuffed olives, pimiento, pickled pepper will all look very pretty, so take your choice.

chinese meat balls

1 pound pork sausage meat
1/4 cup diced onion
1 cup diced celery
1 cup sliced carrots
1-1/2 cups lima beans
1 cup boiling water
1 chicken bouillon cube
2 tablespoons cornstarch
1 tablespoon soy sauce
1/4 cup cold water

Shape sausage into 16 small balls. Brown in heavy skillet. Add onion and cook until tender. Pour off all but 2 tablespoons drippings. Add vegetables. Mix water and bouillon cube. Add to vegetables. Cover and simmer over low heat for 30 minutes to cook vegetables. Blend cornstarch with soy sauce and cold water. Add to hot mixture. Stir til thick. Cook 15 minutes to heat thoroughly. Yield: 4 servings.

MENU: Chinese Meat Balls, Fluffy Rice, Harvard Beets, Molded Fruit Salad, Chocolate Pudding, Beverage.

GARNISH: None needed.

sausage and hominy o'brien

1 pound pork sausage meat
2 tablespoons chopped green pepper
2 tablespoons chopped pimiento
2 tablespoons chopped onion
1 can (16 oz.) golden hominy

Brown and crumble sausage. Remove from skillet and drain all but 3 tablespoons drippings. Brown green pepper, pimiento, and onion in drippings. Add sausage and hominy and heat. Yield: 4 servings.

MENU: Sausage and Hominy O'Brien, Sliced Tomatoes, Buttered Broccoli, Waldorf Salad, Plum Cobbler, Beverage.

GARNISH: None needed.

sausage apple tuckaways

1 pound roll Pork Sausage
1/2 cup chopped apple (1 small)
1-1/2 tablespoons finely chopped celery

Cut sausage into 8 patties. Combine apple and celery. Place 2 tablespoons of apple mixture on four of the patties. Place the other 4 patties on top and pinch the edges together. Cook slowly 25 minutes until brown on both sides and thoroughly cooked. Serve very hot. Yield: 4 servings.

MENU: Sausage Apple Tuckaways, Buttered Spinach, Cottage Fried Potatoes, Red and Green Coleslaw, Gingerbread, Beverage.

Sausage Tuckaways

Make it the same as above except substitute cranberry relish for the apple and chopped celery. This is especially tasty.

sausage loaf and hot applesauce

1 pound of Pork Sausage meat
3 cups bread crumbs
2 eggs
1 teaspoon Worcestershire sauce
1/2 cup sliced stuffed olives

Mix all ingredients. Shape into a loaf. Bake in a preheated 350° oven for 1 hour. Serve with hot applesauce. Yield: 4 servings.

MENU: Sausage Loaf and Hot Applesauce, Oven Browned Potatoes, Brussels Sprouts, Perfection Salad, Butterscotch Pudding, Beverage.

GARNISH: Sprigs of greens or tiny baby beets.

sausage southern

1 pound roll pork sausage
2 tablespoons chopped onion
1 clove garlic, chopped
2 teaspoons brown sugar
1/4 cup catsup
1/4 teaspoon dry mustard
1 can (16 oz.) red kidney beans
1 can (16 oz.) green lima beans
1 tablespoon vinegar

Slice sausage into 10 patties. Brown slowly. Remove sausage and drain off drippings. Brown onion and garlic. Combine onion, garlic, sugar, catsup, mustard, drained kidney beans, drained lima beans and vinegar. Put in a buttered 2-quart casserole. Place sausage on top. Cook uncovered in a preheated 350° oven for 45 minutes or until brown and bubbly. Yield: 5 servings.

MENU: Sausage Southern, Buttered Hominy, Cooked Carrot Sticks, Tomato Aspic, Apple Pie with Cheddar Cheese, Beverage.

GARNISH: Sliced ripe olives.

tomato, kraut and sausage casserole

1 pound roll pork sausage
1/3 cup finely chopped onion
1 can (10-1/2 oz.) condensed tomato soup
1 can (28 oz.) sauerkraut
1 teaspoon Worcestershire sauce
1/4 teaspoon dried basil

Crumble and brown sausage in a heavy skillet. Add onion and brown. Drain off fat. Add remaining ingredients. Mix well. Put in a buttered 2-quart casserole. Bake in a preheated 350° oven for 45 minutes. Yield: 4 servings.

MENU: Tomato Kraut and Sausage Casserole, Parsley Buttered Potatoes, Buttered Green Beans, Prune and Cottage Cheese Salad, Bread Pudding with Lemon Sauce, Beverage.

GARNISH: Use a few cherry tomatoes with a few leaves of green basil, if you have them.

sausage pineapple stack-ups

1 pound pork sausage meat
4 slices canned pineapple
2 teaspoons Dijon mustard
1/4 cup pineapple syrup

Shape sausage into 4 patties a little larger than the pineapple slices. Partially cook patties in a skillet. Brown lightly on both sides. Spread pineapple slices lightly with mustard. Put sausage patties on top. Bake in a 400° oven for 30 minutes. Baste during cooking period with pineapple syrup. Yield: 4 servings.

MENU: Sausage Pineapple Stack-Ups, Scalloped Potatoes, Buttered Asparagus, Chef's Salad, Fudge Cup Cakes, Beverage.

GARNISH: Serve Asparagus on plate with Sausage Pineapple Stack-Ups.

sausage potato soup

5 cups sliced uncooked potatoes
2 medium onions, sliced
1-1/2 cups water
1-1/2 teaspoons salt
1/4 teaspoon celery seed
1 pound roll pork sausage
3 tablespoons finely chopped parsley
2-1/2 cups milk

Combine potatoes, onions, water, salt and celery seed. Cover and heat to a boil. Reduce heat and simmer about 25 minutes or until just a few pieces of potato remain in a thick puree. Stir occasionally. At the same time, crumble and brown sausage. Drain. Add sausage and parsley to potatoes. Stir. Heat milk to scalding. Gradually add milk until soup is of desired consistency. Heat to just below boiling. Yield: 6 servings.

MENU: Sausage and Potato Soup, Toasted Cheese Sandwiches, Carrot Sticks, Dill Pickles, Hot Gingerbread, Beverage.

GARNISH: Save some of the chopped parsley and float it at the last minute.

sausage stuffing (for poultry)

1 pound roll pork sausage
1/2 cup chopped onion
1 cup chopped celery
7 cups dry bread cubes
1 can (10-1/2 oz.) condensed cream of mushroom soup
1/2 cup milk
1 tablespoon chopped parsley
1 teaspoon salt
1 teaspoon poultry seasoning

Fry and crumble sausage until brown. Pour off and save drippings. Add onion and celery. Cook until tender. Add drippings and 3 cups bread cubes. Cook until bread cubes are light brown. Combine soup and milk slowly. Heat, but do not boil. Stir constantly until smooth. Add soup mixture to remaining bread cubes. Combine two bread mixtures. Add parsley and seasonings. Stuff turkey just before putting it in the oven. Yield: 9 cups of stuffing for a 10 pound turkey.

tempting pork sausage and sweet potatoes

4 medium sweet potatoes
3/4 cup brown sugar, firmly packed
2 tablespoons dark corn syrup
1/4 cup orange juice
2 tablespoons lemon juice
1 tablespoon grated orange peel
1 pound roll pork sausage

Cook potatoes in boiling water until tender. Peel. Cut into quarters lengthwise. Mix together in a skillet, sugar, syrup, orange juice, lemon juice and orange peel. Heat to a boil. Add potatoes. Cook slowly for 30 minutes, turning frequently. While potato mixture is cooking, make sausage into 8 patties. Fry slowly until well done. Serve sausage and potatoes very hot. Yield: 4 servings.

MENU: Tempting Pork Sausage and Sweet Potatoes, Buttered Brussels Sprouts, Cranberry Sherbet, Pound Cake with Chocolate Sauce, Beverage.

GARNISH: None needed.

sausage patties in fruit sauce on toast

1 pound roll pork sausage
1-1/2 cups fruit cocktail
1 tablespoon brown sugar
1 tablespoon lemon juice
1/2 teaspoon ginger
1-1/2 teaspoons cornstarch
1 tablespoon water
4 slices hot buttered toast

Shape sausage into 8 patties 1/2 inch thick. Brown slowly and thoroughly in heavy skillet. Pour off drippings. Add fruit cocktail with juice, brown sugar, lemon juice and ginger. Cover and simmer 10 minutes. Remove sausage patties to hot platter. Make a smooth paste with cornstarch and cold water. Stir into fruit cocktail. Simmer until thick and smooth. Stir constantly. Place two sausage patties on each slice of toast. Pour fruit cocktail sauce over sausage patties. Serve hot. Yield: 4 servings.

MENU: Sausage Patties In Fruit Sauce On Toast, Potato Chips, Radish Roses, Caramel Custard, Beverage.

GARNISH: Radish Roses, Mint Leaves.

sausage and vegetable pie

1 pound roll pork sausage
1 medium onion, chopped
1 can (10-1/2 oz.) condensed tomato soup
1 can (10-1/2 oz.) condensed vegetable soup
1 can (16 oz.) mixed vegetables
1 package refrigerator biscuits

Crumble and fry sausage and onion until brown. Pour off drippings. Measure back 2 tablespoons drippings. Add soups and vegetables. Heat to boiling. Pour into buttered casserole. Top with biscuits. Bake in a very hot oven 450° for 15 minutes or until biscuits are browned. NOTE: Use the number of biscuits that fit the top of your casserole, and your family's appetite. Yield: 4 servings.

MENU: Sausage And Vegetable Pie, Mashed Potatoes, Orange and Avocado Salad, Toffee Pudding (refrigerator), Beverage.

GARNISH: None needed.

sausage cornbread

1 pound roll pork sausage
1 cup sifted enriched flour
2-1/2 teaspoons baking powder
1 teaspoon salt
3 tablespoons sugar
1 cup yellow cornmeal
1 egg
1 cup milk

Crumble and partially fry sausage. Drain thoroughly. Save drippings. Sift flour, baking powder, salt and sugar together. Add cornmeal. Beat egg lightly. Add milk. Combine liquid and dry ingredients, 3 tablespoons sausage drippings and one half of the sausage. Stir only enough to moisten. Pour into a square 8-inch cake pan which has been greased only on the bottom. Sprinkle remaining sausage over the top. Bake in a preheated 425° oven for 45 minutes. Serve hot with cream gravy, if desired. Yield: 4 servings.

A cream gravy is simply a medium white sauce made with sausage drippings. The pan is greased only on the bottom for extra volume. The batter will be able to cling to the sides better. All cake and muffin tins should be prepared this way.

MENU: Sausage Cornbread With Cream Gravy, Succotash, Buttered Green Cabbage, Tomato Aspic, Mixed Fruit, Beverage.

GARNISH: Spiced Crab Apples and Celery Leaves.

jiffy sausage

1 pound roll pork sausage
2 tablespoons sausage drippings
6 cups coarsely shredded cabbage
1/2 cup vinegar
1 teaspoon sugar
1 teaspoon celery seed

Crumble and brown sausage. Pour off all drippings except for 2 tablespoons. Add cabbage and brown lightly. Add vinegar, sugar and celery seed. Mix thoroughly. Cover and cook slowly for 10 minutes or until cabbage is tender. Yield: 4 servings.

MENU: Jiffy Sausage, Fluffy Rice, Molded Applesauce Salad, Pecan Cake, Beverage.

pork sausage stuffed baked potatoes

5 medium baking potatoes
1 pound roll pork sausage
1/4 cup scalded milk or light cream
1 tablespoon butter or margarine
1 teaspoon salt
2 teaspoons finely chopped onion
1/2 cup shredded cheddar cheese

Wash potatoes. Bake in a 400° oven for 45 minutes or until soft when a fork is stuck in them. Meanwhile, break up sausage and fry until crumbled, browned and well cooked. Drain off drippings. Cut slices from top of potatoes and scoop out. Mash. Add milk, butter and salt. Beat until smooth. Stir in onion and sausage. Fill potato shells with mixture. Sprinkle with cheese. Place in shallow pan on rack. Bake in a 325° oven for 25 minutes or until cheese is brown. Yield: 5 servings.

NOTE: These potatoes can be prepared in the morning, refrigerated, and reheated for a half hour or until hot just before serving. If you have one or two left, wrap them well in freezer foil and freeze. It works just fine.

MENU: Rib Roast of Beef, Pork Sausage Stuffed Baked Potatoes, Asparagus Amandine, Mandarin Orange Molded Salad, Bananas Foster, Beverage.

GARNISH: The potatoes and greens will garnish the roast.

sausage and rice

1 pound roll pork sausage
1 medium onion, sliced
1 cup uncooked rice
4 cups vegetable cocktail juice
1 teaspoon salt

Crumble sausage. Fry sausage and onion until brown. Drain. Add rice, vegetable cocktail juice and salt. Heat to a boil. Reduce heat. Cover tightly. Simmer 25 minutes or until rice is tender. If rice becomes dry, add more vegetable cocktail juice or water. Yield: 4-6 servings.

MENU: Sausage and Rice, Buttered Broccoli, Carrot and Raisin Salad, Chocolate Refrigerator Cake, Beverage.

GARNISH: This looks and tastes like spanish rice. Serve it on a chop plate with the broccoli around it. Small red and yellow pickled peppers would taste good and look very pretty.

sausage cheese bake

1 pound roll pork sausage
2 tablespoons finely chopped green pepper
3/4 cup plus 1/4 cup shredded cheddar cheese
1-1/2 cups medium white sauce
1/2 teaspoon ground rosemary
1/4 teaspoon dry mustard
2 eggs, hard cooked and sliced
1 pkg. (8 oz.) noodles, cooked

Crumble and brown sausage. Drain. Add green pepper and cook slowly until tender. Add 3/4 cup cheese to white sauce. Heat and stir until cheese melts. Mix white sauce, rosemary, mustard, eggs and noodles to sausage. Place in a buttered 2-quart casserole. Sprinkle with 1/4 cup cheese. Bake in a 350° oven for 1 hour. Yield: 4 servings.

MENU: Sausage Cheese Bake, Sliced Tomatoes, Peas and Tiny Onions, Crisp Green Salad, Green Apple Pie, Beverage.

GARNISH: None needed.

sausage cups and baked beans

1 pound lean roll pork sausage
1 can (16 oz.) pork and beans
1/2 cup tangy catsup

Line 8 sections of a muffin tin with sausage meat. Fill with beans and top each cup with one tablespoon catsup. Place in a preheated 400° oven for 30 minutes. Serve very hot. Yield: 4 servings.

MENU: Sausage Cups and Baked Beans, Buttered Carrot Sticks, Sauteed Zucchini, Mixed Raw Vegetable Salad, Butterscotch Pudding, Beverage.

GARNISH: Serve carrots on the platter with the Sausage Cups and garnish with cherry tomatoes sliced half way down and dabbed with some cheese spread.

not much time casserole

1 package precooked smoked pork sausage
1 can (16 oz.) whole kernel yellow corn
1 can (2 oz.) mushrooms
1 can (10-1/2 oz.) condensed tomato soup
Dash pepper

Cut half sausage into half inch pieces. Drain corn and mushrooms. Combine all ingredients except remaining sausages. Pour into a buttered 2-quart casserole. Top with whole sausages. Bake in a preheated 400° oven for 15 minutes with cover on and 5 minutes with cover off. Yield: 4 servings.

MENU: Not Much Time Casserole, Creamed Green Beans, Pickled Beets and Hard Cooked Egg Salad, Chocolate Sundae, Beverage.

GARNISH: None needed.

quickie pizza

1 package precooked smoked pork sausage
4 hamburger buns
8 teaspoons butter or margarine
8 tablespoons chili sauce
1 cup shredded mozzarella cheese
1/8 teaspoon oregano
1/8 teaspoon basil

Cut sausage into halves lengthwise and crosswise. Cut buns in halves. Toast both halves. Spread with butter and chili sauce. Put one sausage on each bun half. Top with cheese. Sprinkle with herbs. Bake in a preheated 400° oven for 10 minutes. Yield: 4 servings.

MENU: Quickie Pizza, Corn Chips, Pickles, Carrot Sticks, Celery Sticks, Beverage.

sausage and cranberry-orange

1 package precooked Smoked Pork Sausage links
1 cup cranberry-orange relish
1/4 cup water

Heat sausage according to directions. Add relish and water. Heat together. Serve hot relish with sausage. Yield: 4 servings.

Cranberry-Orange Relish

1 quart cranberries (1 pound)
1 large orange and peel
2/3 cup sugar

Put cranberries through food chopper or in blender. Quarter orange and remove seeds. Put through the food chopper or blender. Add sugar and blend until dissolved. Chill at least 3 hours to blend flavors. Yield: 2-1/2 cups.

MENU: Sausage and Cranberry-Orange, Whipped Potatoes, Green Peas, Cabbage Salad, Butterscotch Pudding, Beverage.

GARNISH: Celery Leaves.

smoked sausage and candied pineapple

1 package precooked Smoked Pork Sausage Links
2 cups pineapple chunks, drained
1/2 cup brown sugar, firmly packed

Heat sausage according to directions on package. Remove sausage from skillet. Keep warm. Blend sugar with drippings in skillet. Add pineapple. Cook 5 minutes or until pineapple is browned. Serve pineapple and sausage together. Yield: 4 servings.

MENU: Smoked Country Sausage and Candied Pineapple, Potato Puffs, Buttered Mixed Vegetables, Green Salad, Strawberry Ice Cream, Beverage.

GARNISH: None needed.

smoked country sausage and cornbread

1 pound smoked country sausage
Packaged cornbread mix

Place sausage in a shallow baking dish (10 x 6 x 2). Bake in a preheated 375° oven for 10 minutes. Turn sausage and bake for an additional 5 minutes. Brush sides of dish with drippings. Remove excess drippings and save. Increase oven temperature to 475°. Leave sausage in oven. Prepare cornbread according to directions. Pour over sausage. Bake for 20 to 25 minutes or until cornbread is cooked. Serve with cream gravy made with drippings. Yield: 4 to 5 servings.

MENU: Smoked Country Sausage and Cornbread, Sauteed Cherry Tomatoes, Peas and Onions, Red and Green Slaw, Apple Dumplings, Beverage.

GARNISH: None needed.

smoked country sausage and poached pineapple slices

1 pound smoked country sausage links
1/4 cup water
6 slices pineapple
1/4 cup cinnamon candy drops

Put sausage and water in skillet. Cover and steam for five minutes. Pour off liquid and cook sausages slowly for 25 minutes or until thoroughly cooked and golden brown. Remove sausages from skillet and keep hot in oven. Remove all but 2 tablespoons drippings from pan. Add 1/4 cup hot water. Melt candies in fat and water, stirring constantly. Poach pineapple in mixture for 10 minutes. Place sausage through each pineapple ring and serve. Yield: 6 servings.

MENU: Smoked Country Sausage and Poached Pineapple Slices, Buttered Broccoli, Creamed Potatoes, Three Bean Salad, Cherry Turnovers, Beverage.

GARNISH: None needed.

herbs

There are many herbs that are available dried or ground in stores. Many of these herbs can be grown in pots in your kitchen or in your yard. Naturally, fresh herbs like anything else that is fresh, taste best. If you use commercially prepared herbs like most of us do, try to keep their original strength by using them within 6 months or a year. If your herbs or spices are in large containers, keep them in a cool place and keep the jars tightly covered. Some herbs, like onion and garlic powders, and salts, paprika and mustards keep best in the refrigerator.

Here are a few that are especially good with pork. Incidentally, there are only two rules that are important to remember when using herbs:

1. Use a very small amount to point up, not cover up the flavor of the pork.
2. If you like the herb with pork, use it. Don't be bound by lists like the following.

Basil. A flavor that is associated with Italian tomato sauce. 1/4 teaspoon dried basil for 4 servings or 1 teaspoon of the fresh herb will be a good starting point.

Bay Leaf. This is the laurel leaf and even the dried herb is potent. Start with a third or even a quarter of a leaf for stews or sauces. Always remove the bay leaf before serving. It has been said that a whole dried bay leaf laid on the back of closet shelves will keep silverfish away. It's worth trying.

Capers. These are the pickled flower buds of a wild European plant. They are slightly salty and are delightful when used in sauces like sour cream. About a teaspoon for salad or sauce for 4 is right.

Celery. Nearly everyone knows about celery salt and seed, but do they remember the leaves? They are so tasty when finely chopped and sauteed for hot foods or when used cold for salads, sandwich spreads, etc. One teaspoon of chopped, fresh celery leaves for a service of four is right. Celery leaves are also very attractive when used as green garnish around meat.

Chervil. This isn't seen fresh very often in the United States but is available dried and tastes much like parsley but is slightly more peppery. Try a quarter teaspoon per 4 servings of the dried variety.

Chives. These pretty little spikes with the pink clover-like blossoms are just as happy growing in pots in your window as in your backyard. They are also available dried or frozen. They have, as you know, a mild onion-like flavor and a lovely bright green color. I'm sure you know how much you and your family like to use in your food.

Comino. This is sometimes known as cumin and is the flavor not the heat in chili powder. It is used in nearly all meat dishes in Mexico. The Germans sometimes use it in place of caraway. It's potent! Try an 1/8 teaspoon at first to see how you like it.

Coriander. This has an unusual flavor unless you remember the center of the "jaw breakers" from your penny candy days. That was coriander and it is used by many to combine with sage to rub on ham and fresh pork before roasting. Try equal parts of sage and coriander.

Dill. Dill seed and dill pickles are well known but dill weed is just beginning to build popularity. Use it just about any way you like but remember that it is dried and concentrated. 1/4 teaspoon for four will be properly elusive.

Garlic. The salt and powder should be kept in the refrigerator to maintain the strength. Use the salt in a dish that needs to be salted also. Use the powder when you only want garlic flavor. 1/8 teaspoon will work just fine. Garlic juice is available in most markets. It is very easy to use but add it by drops until you get used to it. Dried garlic cloves are available and take a little extra trouble but many think it's worth it. Of course it is the most reasonable.

Ginger. People all but choose sides with this spice and it's a shame because it does some wonderful things for many foods, fresh pork included. Try just a sprinkle or two in a fruit sauce and taste the results.

Horseradish. This is actually aggressive but when used with tart foods like salad dressings or in mustards or meat sauces it is quite tasty. Years ago fine restaurants used to serve curls of fresh grated horseradish with roasts. It was comparatively mild and delicious.

continued on next page

Mace is the stronger covering of nutmeg. It is used in pork sausage as well as in meat loaves. Use it sparingly.

Marjoram. This is one of the delightful backyard herbs that is tasty in salads, sauces, chops, wherever you want a nice fresh green herb flavor. Oregano and marjoram have a somewhat similar flavor though marjoram is more mild. 1/4 to 1/2 teaspoon of the dried herb is a good amount to use.

Mint is so common that it hardly needs mentioning. Yet many never think of using it for pork or for a garnish.

Mustard. There is dry and dry hot mustard and they are both excellent with fresh as well as with smoked pork. One thing, let any sauce with dry mustard in it stand for an hour or two. Prepared mustards are varied also. Do you know the French Dijon? It's made with white wine and is delightful. The German Dusseldorf is a little stronger but is great for stronger flavored foods. There are a number of other styles of mustard so do be adventurous.

Nutmeg. This is also used in sausages as well as in pure pork sausage. Try blending a very little bit in the sauce for the chops.

Parsley. Try chopping parsley very fine to use in salad dressings and sauces. The mustard sauce in the German recipe is a good example.

Pepper. There are several kinds that are used for different tastes. The black and the white pepper come from the same berry. The *black pepper* is the whole berry and is the most pungent. The white pepper comes from the inside of the berry and is a little milder. In many of the recipes for fresh pork in the front of the book, we recommended white pepper so that it wouldn't show. Cayenne and red pepper come from different varieties of capsicum. All of which add up to the fact that both varieties are hot and should be used only to point up a flavor.

Poultry Seasoning. This is a combination of herbs and spices meant originally for poultry stuffing. It's too good to be used for just one purpose. Try it with fresh pork right along with salt and pepper. You'll enjoy it.

Rosemary. This is very close to sage in flavor, but is different enough to be tasty in salads and sauces. The needles should be ground into small pieces. A whole needle of rosemary is not too welcome to find in one's food. We keep a separate pepper mill to grind things like rosemary and dill seed. Use about 1/8 to 1/4 teaspoon per four servings.

Sage. This is known primarily as the herb used in poultry stuffing, however, particularly in the south, it is also used extensively in pork sausage. Sage is a tasty herb, particularly when it is used fresh. Unfortunately, it has been overused so much that it has lots of enemies. Start with an eighth of a teaspoon for four servings and be sure that you never increase it to the point where your family can identify it.

Savory. This herb is known as the string bean herb because it is used so often in this combination. However, try sprinkling some minced fresh or dried savory over ham or other smoked pork just before serving it. Savory would be another candidate for the extra pepper mill referred to in the Rosemary paragraph.

Seasoned Salt. This is the convenience flavoring because it is a combination of salt, paprika, garlic, onion and other flavors. A dash or two of this and your flavoring job is over. There are several varieties of this on the market. Use your favorite.

Tarragon. Sharp, pungent or any other like term could be used to describe this favorite of the French. It must be used in combination with several other flavorings and a minimum must be used, but it is delightful.

Thyme. This is my favorite of all the herbs. It's much milder than sage but can be used the same way. Use it in stuffings, salads, sauces or just to chop or grind over the pork just before serving. It is also very pretty as a border in the garden.

Watercress. I can't think of a single place where this wouldn't be beautiful and tasty unless it would be for dessert. Serve it to garnish the roast or chops, use it in a cream soup, a salad, a dip or a spread or in a sauce.

glossary

a la Goldenrod—served with chopped hard cooked egg white topped with sieved hard cooked yolk.

Amandine—To serve something with brown butter with and in which toasted slivered almonds have been browned.

Bake—To cook in oven, with meats it is usually used interchangeably. A distinction could be made that baking meat is to cook covered and roasting meat is to cook uncovered. This is an excellent example of splitting hairs.

Bananas Foster—This is a spectacular flaming dessert made popular by the famous Brennan's Restaurant in New Orleans. It is made with bananas, brown sugar, rum, banana liqueur and ice cream.

Baste—To spoon or pour liquid over a food as it is cooking.

Bavarian Cream—A fruit flavored dessert made of gelatin with beaten egg white and/or whipped cream folded in. It is especially pretty and appealing if fresh fruit is served around it.

Blend—To combine to make a uniform mixture.

Bouillon—a fatless broth of chicken or beef extracted flavors.

Braise—To brown meat in a small amount of fat and then continue cooking covered in a small amount of liquid until tender.

Bread Crumbs—Fine—This means that the bread has been dried and then rolled and preferably sifted. Soft—This means that the bread is fresh and that little pieces are torn out of the center.

Catsup, tangy—There are many flavors of catsup—sweet, spicy, fruity and tangy. Tangy catsup has a slightly hot, horseradish taste.

Cherry Tomatoes—Small tomatoes about 1 inch in diameter. These seem to taste more "home grown" in winter than the larger varieties.

Chinese Cabbage—This has the shape of romaine, and the color of cabbage and celery. The top looks like cabbage and the bottom looks like celery. It tastes like a combination of the two. It is marvelous as a salad. Mix it with other greens or cut it crosswise about 1 inch thick and serve with French dressing.

Cinnamon Apple Slices—These are slices of apple, usually cut crosswise, that are poached until tender in a cinnamon candy and water solution.

Cinnamon Candies—These are the little bright red cinnamon candies that everyone used to call red hots.

Collops—These are very thin slices of meat that are cooked very quickly in butter or olive oil and served with a simple sauce like lemon.

Cranberry-Orange Relish—This is the uncooked mixture of raw cranberries and unpeeled orange that is ground and sweetened.

Cream or Milk Gravy—a gravy made just like medium white sauce and using the meat fat for flavoring.

Crepes—These are very thin pancakes that are usually filled and rolled. Sometimes they are folded in quarters and served with a sauce. They may be for main course or for dessert. They are French in usage and name.

Croutons—Small cubes of bread that are fried or toasted in butter. They are used in salads and as garnishes.

Curry Powder—A combination of seasonings that originated in India. Every curry powder differs in intensity so when you find your favorite brand, stick by it.

Drippings—The fat that drips from the meat as it cooks.

Flan—A baked custard that is made in most of the Spanish-speaking countries. It usually has caramelized sugar in the bottom of the baking dish so that it forms a sauce when turned out of the dish. There is a French flän that is like a shallow tart and is made in a typical fluted pan.

Glazed—Cooked in a thin sugar syrup to coat the product as it cooks or after it is cooked.

Grand Marnier Sauce—A cornstarch thickened sauce flavored with Grand Marnier, an orange flavored liqueur.

Green Noodles—Ordinary egg noodles that have had pureed spinach mixed into the dough before rolling, cutting and drying. They are a very pretty color and have a good flavor. Some companies just call them spinach noodles.

Hominy—This is corn that has been processed to be puffed almost like popcorn. It is available in white or gold and is very tasty when heated and served with butter. Sometimes we mash it, add shredded Swiss cheese, light cream and butter and bake it. Guests compliment us on the delicious mashed potatoes.

Julienne—Cut into very fine strips.

Kohlrabi—A vegetable that is green like a cabbage, about the size of a turnip and has leaves on long stems that grow right out of the sides. Dice or slice them and cook in a little water and butter or in cream sauce.

Kumquats—Small citrus fruit that have edible skins and bitter pulp. They are usually preserved and are delightful.

Lyonnaise Potatoes—Sliced fried potatoes with onions and sprinkled with chopped parsley.

Mandarin Oranges—Tiny tangerine-like oranges. They are available in cans in most areas.

Minced—Chopped very fine.

Mozzarella cheese—a semisoft mild cheese that is used for pizza and for other recipes that require a non-stringing cheese.

Paprika—A bright red sweet pepper that is used for garnishing by Americans and for flavoring by Hungarians.

Perfection Salad—A molded Cabbage and green pepper sweet sour salad.

Poach—To cook in liquid very slowly so the product will not lose its shape. The liquid is frequently spooned onto the top of the product being cooked.

Ragout—A meat stew.

continued on next page

Roly Poly—A fruit or berry dessert that is made by rolling sweetened fruit in a very rich and soft biscuit dough. The roll is about 15 inches long and about 4 to 6 inches across. The dough is so soft and rich that it breaks in spots and the fruit oozes out as it cooks. It is served warm with cream to hungry children with hollow legs.

Rosette—A sprig of greens that are full and rose-like.

Saute—To brown quickly in fat.

Scoring—To cut the fat for decoration as with a ham, or for tenderness as with a flank steak.

Shred—To tear or cut into very fine pieces.

Simmer—To cook with the liquid below the boiling temperature.

Snow Peas—A special variety of peas that are used by the Oriental people. The pods are so tender that they are eaten just like green beans.

Steam—To cook a product in a covered pan in a very small amount of water so that most of the cooking is done by steam. The link pork sausages are cooked for 5 minutes by steam.

Succotash—A combination of green lima beans and yellow whole kernel corn. It was supposedly taught to the pilgrims by the Indians.

Sunshine Salad—A molded gelatin salad with crushed pineapple and shredded carrots.

Tomato Aspic—A gelatin salad made of tomato juice simmered with chopped onion, celery, and green pepper and seasoned to taste. It is then strained and poured into individual molds for luncheon.

Vegetable Cocktail Juice—A canned product made of tomato juice, celery, onion, green pepper and other juices and seasonings. When combined with gelatin, it makes a good aspic.

Water Chestnuts—These look like small potatoes when the cans are opened. They are usually sliced and used in Chinese-type foods or in casseroles. Their purpose is to provide a crisp texture.

Wax Beans—yellow string beans. They have the same flavor but sometimes add color interest.

Wine, dry—this means a sour wine or one that lacks sweetness. This is good to use in cooking, for an appetizer, salad, fish, meat or vegetable.

index

equivalents and substitutions

3 teaspoons = 1 tablespoon
4 tablespoons = 1/4 cup
5-1/3 tablespoons = 1/3 cup
8 tablespoons = 1/2 cup
10-2/3 tablespoons = 2/3 cup
12 tablespoons = 3/4 cup
16 tablespoons = 1 cup

2 tablespoons = 1 fluid ounce
4 tablespoons = 1/4 cup = 2 fluid ounces
8 tablespoons = 1/2 cup = 4 fluid ounces

2 cups = 1 pint
2 pints = 1 quart
4 quarts = 1 gallon

1 tablespoon cornstarch = 2 tablespoons flour
1 cup milk = 1/2 cup evaporated milk plus 1/2 cup water
1 pound shredded cheddar or process cheese = 4 cups
Juice of 1 lemon = 3 to 4 tablespoons
Juice of 1 orange = 6 to 7 tablespoons
Grated peel of 1 lemon = 1 teaspoon
Grated peel of 1 orange = 2 teaspoons
1 medium apple, chopped = 1 cup
1 medium onion, chopped = 1/2 cup
20 salted crackers = 1 cup fine crumbs
2 tablespoons butter = 1 ounce
1 stick butter = 1/4 pound = 1/2 cup
1 pound ground uncooked ham = about 3 cups
1 pound ground cooked ham = about 3-1/2 cups
4 ounces uncooked macaroni = 1 to 1-1/4 cups = 2-1/4 cups cooked
4 ounces uncooked noodles = 1-1/2 to 2 cups = 2-1/2 cups cooked
4 ounces uncooked spaghetti = 1 to 1-1/2 cups = 2-1/2 cups cooked
6-1/2 to 7 ounces uncooked rice = 1 cup = 3 to 3-1/2 cups cooked